Sleep

I dedicate this book to my darling children and grandchildren. You all mean so much to me and without you I would not have been able to write this book. To my son Ben and his wife Helen, their children Hannah and Jessica; my daughter Sarah, her husband Reuben, their children Zack, Bethany and Joshua; my daughter Jayne and her fiancé Peter: thank you for your encouragement to press on and keep writing. I hope that this will be a practical and timeless guide which you can offer to friends and families to help with all-important sleep in the years to come.

Sleep

solutions

**Quiet nights for you and your child:
from birth to five years**

RACHEL WADDILOVE

LION

Published by Lion Books
an imprint of
Lion Hudson plc
Wilkinson House, Jordan Hill Road,
Oxford OX2 8DR, England
www.lionhudson.com/lion

ISBN 978 0 7459 5573 5
e-ISBN 978 0 7459 5760 9

First edition 2013

A catalogue record for this book is available from the British Library

Printed and bound in Great Britain, December 2012, LH26

Contents

Acknowledgments

I am grateful to Stuart Logan, Professor of Paediatric Epidemiology at Exeter University Medical School, for his time and expertise in reading the book and for writing such a warm Foreword. I would also like to say a huge thank you to my dear friends Stuart and Sue Mountford who provided their lovely home in Cornwall as an oasis where I could go to plan and write this book. Sue, being with you again took me back to our college days and all the fun we had together. Thank you so much for feeding me, continually bringing me cups of tea and coffee and a gin and tonic at the end of the writing day. I couldn't have done it without you!

To my dear friend Naomi Gilbert, who once again has stood beside me and guided me as I have written, thank you so much. Nay, it's been great to work together again.

I want to say a huge thank you to the mums who have taken time to write case studies for me. This has helped to bring warmth and reality to each chapter. I so appreciate you being willing to share your unique stories of sleep problems and solutions.

Thank you to each and every family who has invited me into their home or called me for advice on their children's sleep. I couldn't have written this book without you. You have given me such a breadth of experience in the problems and challenges we can all face with our children's sleep. It has been a privilege to work with such lovely families right across the country and overseas.

Thank you to Ali Hull and Rhoda Hardie at Lion Hudson for all your encouragement.

Last but not least, to my dear husband John – thank you for your support and for keeping the home fires burning while I disappeared to Cornwall to write. Thank you for your encouragement to write another book.

Foreword

Being a parent is the most enjoyable thing I have ever done but it is also the most difficult. It sometimes seems strange that being a parent can be so challenging when it is such a normal part of life for every generation. When I was a young paediatrician talking to families about sleep problems, I often found it difficult to understand why they found it so hard to follow my advice. Once I had children of my own I suddenly understood.

Every child is different and all childhood behaviours are the result of a complex dance between parents and children to which all parties contribute. Children are very sensitive to their parents' emotions and parents to those of their children. It can be very easy to get stuck in unhelpful patterns of interaction, although driven by the best of intentions – especially when you are exhausted from lack of sleep.

In our modern society, most of us come to parenting with very little experience. Even fifty years ago families were much larger and most people lived closer to their extended families. This led to children growing up with much more first-hand experience of babies and small children than the parents of today. It's a staggering thought to realize that, for the first time in history, over fifty per cent of children in our society are firstborns. Geographical dispersion of families also means that many parents have less access to advice and, more importantly, less access to people who can provide emotional and practical support when things are difficult.

All of this means that as parents we need different ways of getting help. Rachel Waddilove brings a wealth of experience and expertise to her writing. She is both a parent, a grandparent, and a professional working with young children. This enables her to speak with an understanding of both the science and the reality of parenting. This book builds on her excellent previous books about babies and toddlers to concentrate on dealing with sleeping, perhaps the most overwhelming challenge for parents of young children. It offers useful answers to the questions that often plague parents, such as how much sleep is "normal" at different ages. Most importantly, though, it offers practical ways of preventing and dealing with difficulties. The arrangement into chapters based on age seems to me a sensible way of ensuring that the advice is specific enough to be really helpful.

Combining warmth and practicality, this is a book I am happy to recommend to parents.

Professor Stuart Logan
Cerebra Professor of Paediatric Epidemiology
University of Exeter Medical School

Introduction

How many times do we hear the comment, when telling people that we are having a baby, "That's the last time you'll have a good night's sleep for a very long time!" Somehow it seems to be expected that having a baby or bringing up young children includes sleepless nights as part of the package. Of course we know that to a certain point this is true, as new babies need to be fed regularly through the night. However, in my experience, as long as baby is fit and healthy and having enough milk, he or she can and will sleep through the night from quite a young age.

I am the eldest of six children. There are ten years between me and my youngest sibling so I cannot remember a time when there wasn't a baby in the home. I went off to college to train as a nursery nurse at the age of seventeen and went on to work with families until I married. After raising three children, I went back to working with families some years ago. I now have five grandchildren who are all growing up and at school, and they are a real delight to be with and such fun.

I am writing this book as, after years of experience with families, I know so well how vital it is for babies and children to sleep. I feel desperately sad for parents whose children don't sleep well. Many parents who call me for advice on sleep problems are at the end of their tether and don't know what to do next. This is a horrid position to be in, but so often you just need help and encouragement to get you through this stage.

But before I go into detail about babies and children sleeping, let's look a little at the whole subject of sleep.

Sleep is important for everyone, at any age. It can also be an issue at any time of life. Sleep is essential for growth of the body and mind, and for one's general well-being. We all know that if we are sleep deprived we don't function as well as we do when we have slept well. However, it is amazing how little sleep we can survive on as new mums and dads. Often mums will say to me they don't know how they are managing to function with so little sleep, but they do.

I know the same feeling. Having done years of maternity work and being up with newborns in the night I am amazed sometimes at my energy levels. But I do know that we can get very stressed about not having enough sleep, and of course the more we worry about not sleeping the worse it is. We suffer from that horrid feeling of being exhausted when we go to bed, but not being able to drop off. Our bodies are so tense and wired, sleep just doesn't come.

Babies need sleep for their bodies and brains to develop and for their general well-being. Toddlers too need sleep, especially when they are running around all day. When your baby becomes a toddler he may start waking in the night and then be very grumpy in the day. We will cover this in detail in the sections of the book dealing with the toddler years. Preschool and school age children, especially, also need to sleep well. Children who go to school without enough sleep will underachieve in class. Ask any teacher of four- to six-year-olds, and they will point out to you the children who don't have good sleeping patterns. Their levels of concentration are very poor and often they are not very happy at school because they are so tired.

What happens when our children get to the teenage years? Isn't it funny that we spend years trying to get our children to sleep on in the mornings and then when they become teenagers we can't get them out of bed? We know that they need more sleep through those years, even though they often go to bed much later. Their body clocks seem to change somewhat, meaning they can easily stay up all night and sleep for most of the day.

Of course, adults with young children need lots of sleep. I remember when I had a young family my head would touch the pillow at night and I would sleep deeply till the morning.

Most of my clients who call for advice want to know how to deal with a baby or child who doesn't sleep. There are different methods of sleep training babies and young children and some quite strong opinions on how it should be done. I use either the "controlled crying" or the "shout it out" methods of sleep training, but I acknowledge that some parents find these methods difficult to implement. Don't worry if you think you are approaching the problem too late. It is never too late; it is just easier if you are able to teach your child how to sleep well at an early age.

This book is a guide for parents of newborns through to five-year-olds and may seem quite repetitive as each chapter covers a different age group. Each chapter contains advice on how to ensure baby settles well from the start, and a troubleshooting section you can refer to when things aren't going smoothly. You can either read the book straight through or go immediately to the chapter that covers the age that is most relevant to your needs. I suggest you do the latter if you are desperate to teach your baby or child to sleep through the night. I have always referred to baby as "he", but this is just for convenience and to avoid confusion. All the advice, suggestions, and comments in this book apply equally to girls and boys.

My hope is that you will be able to put into practice some of the advice I give, find it helpful as a family, and then enjoy plenty of good, peaceful nights' sleep!

The importance of sleep

During the last weeks of pregnancy you will probably not have slept well at all, due to your size and baby moving around at night. Try to get as much rest as you can in the day and get your feet up when possible. This is easier if you don't have a toddler running around. If you do have a little one with lots of energy, try to find a friend or family member who can take him off your hands for an hour or so here and there. If you don't have anyone around to help, then while you put your feet up on the sofa put a DVD on for your little one, perhaps a special one for rest times. Tuck him up with you for half an hour or so. He will soon get into the habit of doing this. If he is still resting in the day, put your feet up while he naps.

You will very likely be tired after giving birth, particularly if you have had a long-drawn-out labour, as this can be physically exhausting. Many women are amazed at how tired they do feel in those early weeks. Your hormone levels will be up and down and you may feel all over the place emotionally – tired and tearful and unable to sleep. This is quite normal after giving birth.

If you are breastfeeding, this too can make you feel emotional, especially if you struggle to get going or it is painful. Don't be afraid to ask your midwife to help you with feeding. Many women need help and advice with this for several weeks. It is such an important part of a baby's life, as if he isn't feeding well, he won't sleep well. Don't say no to family and friends who offer to come and help.

Another reason for tiredness is that you will have broken nights with baby needing to feed. Sometimes he just doesn't seem to settle down to sleep again as easily as he does in the day. Things always seem worse at night. I will talk about this in the next chapter.

So, tiredness is inevitable after giving birth, but it doesn't mean you can't rest in the day. Do feed baby on your bed with your feet up whenever you can and then have a nap when baby is sleeping. The hormone oxytocin that is released by breastfeeding helps you to feel sleepy, and many mums will nap after a feed. The best way is to have baby's cot by your bed. When you have winded and changed him, just tuck him in his cot. You can sleep while he does.

Do remember that lack of sleep will affect how you feel during the day. It is so easy to be grumpy and think you are never going to feel normal again. You may be surprised to feel like this if this is your first baby, so it is important that you can chat about it with your partner and family and understand why you may be out of sorts with each other.

Impact of sleep on family life

Everyone needs to know how to wind down, as this helps us to sleep well. It is important to teach our babies and children how to do this, as the whole family will benefit from having restful nights.

Before you have a family you may not know how shattering sleep deprivation can be. Fortunately it is only for a while: things do pass and baby will grow up and learn to sleep. This is a fact you need to hold onto. It is well known that lack of sleep for mum may be one of the contributory factors to postnatal depression, especially if she has a tendency to depression already. This of course will have an effect on the whole family.

It is so important to talk with your partner and health professional. If you don't, misunderstandings can become much worse. Sleep deprivation is a killer for relationships, as it makes everyone cross and irritable with each other. If you have other children, it has an effect on them too. They will become grumpy because you are tired and have no patience. All you want to do is go to bed and sleep for weeks.

So if this is what you are going through as a family, you need a plan. The list below contains some ideas and suggestions you might like to try if you have a new baby and are suffering with tiredness.

1. Talk about it together.

2. Make sure you rest with your feet up once in the day. Go back to bed after baby's early morning feed.

3. Make time to have a soak in a bath or take a long shower.

4. Have a night off at weekends, asking your partner to do the night feed. This is easier to arrange if your baby will take a bottle of formula or expressed breast milk.

5. Ask mum or a friend to come in and help with practical things.

6. Ask friends to make a main meal for you whenever they can in the early days. Often feeding ourselves is the last thing we want to do!

7. If you have other children who are at nursery or school, ask someone to do the school run for a while. Most mothers are happy to help as they have been there too.

8. Spend some time together as a couple: either have a take away or go out for lunch or supper. This will benefit your relationship and will also help you to be more relaxed and sleep well.

9. If you are having problems with sleeping, do talk to your doctor and she may give you something to help you sleep. Insomnia is quite common after giving birth.

If, as a new mum, you feel particularly anxious and stressed when your baby cries, nothing you do seems to work and you feel out of control, do get some help. If your partner, mum, or a friend can take care of baby while you have a breather for a little while, this will help the situation. I will talk more about this later in the book.

What should I expect as a new parent?

New parents often ask, "When can I expect to have a good night's sleep again?" It is a myth that some children are born bad sleepers. I want to assure you that you can have good nights from early on. However, you will have broken nights at times even if your child or children are the best sleepers. In the early days this is inevitable, as new babies need to be fed. But this will pass. Later on, as babies get older, they can be ill, or have teeth coming through, or they may have dreams and nightmares that wake them up. Coping with this is all part of parenting. Having said that, if you are willing to persevere and are lovingly consistent with your baby or child, you can teach them to sleep from an early age. Babies, children, and parents all thrive when they sleep well.

Teaching your child to sleep is just one aspect of good parenting. It is part of teaching your child boundaries. Today many parents seem to feel afraid to set boundaries, whether for sleep or behaviour. Parenting is a big responsibility that brings with it all sorts of ups and downs: it is the most important and valuable job you will ever do in your life. However, I want to encourage you to remember that when the going is tough and you are shattered and worn out, it is just for a season. Your child will grow up and he will respond to the love, care, and boundaries that you are giving him.

Sleep solutions: from birth to three months

The earlier you can get baby sleeping well, the better it is for everyone. Some babies sleep better than others and it is harder to teach some little ones to sleep than others. But it is always worth it. You don't need to lay down hard and fast rules but you do need to gently and lovingly establish good sleeping patterns. It is so much better for baby if he learns to settle himself and sleep well.

You may well find that baby sleeps for quite a few hours after birth, perhaps even through his first night, and you are thrilled, thinking that you have got a sleeping baby. Very often, once newborns have been fed they do sleep well. But you may find that as soon as you get home, which could be anything from six hours to three days later, depending on where you deliver and what sort of delivery you have had, your baby doesn't stop shouting. The little person you had in hospital becomes someone very different when you get him home, and you just don't seem to be able to pacify him. Don't worry if this is the case – it's a common experience. In this chapter I am going to look at how to settle your baby and get him into a good sleeping pattern.

How much sleep does a newborn need?

Babies need about sixteen to eighteen hours' sleep in every twenty-four hours in their first few weeks.

A newborn baby will normally feed and then go straight back to sleep again. He may follow that pattern all day, and probably most of the night too. If baby was born early he will probably sleep his way through the days until he comes to his due date, when he may suddenly wake up and you wonder what has happened. One of our children was born two weeks early and hardly woke at all. I was beginning to worry that there was something wrong with her, when she suddenly woke up on her due date and definitely let us know that she was there!

New parents often ask if their baby really needs to sleep in the day as well as at night. It's tempting to think that if you keep baby awake during the day, he will sleep better at night. However, your baby does need daytime sleeps as well as sleep at night-time. In fact, keeping him awake in the day can make his night-time sleeping worse. The better the daytime sleep he gets, the more settled baby will be at night. In some funny way, sleep produces sleep.

New babies may not sleep well after every feed. Even if they are mostly very settled, you may find that after one particular feed they are wakeful and will hardly settle until after the next feed. This usually happens after the early evening feed, at about 6 to 7 p.m.

Where should my baby sleep?

The current advice given to all parents is for your baby to sleep in your bedroom, as close as possible to you, for the first six months of his life. When I am working as a maternity nurse I always have baby by the side of my bed all night. This is really for the mother's peace of mind, but it is also so that I can feed him in the night without disturbing anyone else in the house. Having said this, if I have an en suite bathroom that is big enough for the cot, after a few nights I may move baby into the bathroom, especially if he is a noisy sleeper. However, when our own children were babies none of them slept in our room when I came home from hospital with them. They were near to us in another bedroom and I kept both bedroom doors open so that we could hear them easily when they woke needing to be fed.

Many parents ask when they can move baby to his own room. If baby is fit and healthy in every way you can move him to his own room as soon as you feel ready to let him go. I personally feel that six months is far too long to keep him in your room; baby is disturbed by you and you are disturbed by his little noises in the night. If you are trying to sleep train your baby or young toddler they need to be in their own room, as it is impossible to do it with them in the same bedroom as you.

Having said all of this, it is up to you as a parent to move baby when you feel ready. Lots of parents move baby out when he is about one month old. This seems a sensible time to me, as usually by then baby is starting to sleep for longer at night.

Baby should not sleep in bed with you. The risks of baby suffocating are high and the FSID (The Foundation for the Study of Infant Deaths) advice is not to co-sleep. I know it is tempting when you are tired to bring baby into bed with you, but it is not recommended.

Monitors

Do you need a baby monitor? Most families use monitors these days and in general they are very helpful, especially if you have a large house. I have recently used a monitor with a screen so that you can see what baby is doing as well as hear him. I was sceptical about this at first, but it was quite useful to see that baby was asleep and settled. However, be careful that you don't become fixated with the monitor and jump up at every little noise to check what baby is doing. This really isn't healthy.

What should my baby sleep in?

There are many different cots and cribs to choose from for your new baby. You don't need to spend lots of money on a first-size cot, as baby will grow out of it quite quickly. Some parents borrow a small cot or Moses basket from friends. However, it is usually a good idea to buy a new mattress. Whatever size or shape cot you are borrowing, make sure that it is safe and secure and will hold your child when he can stand up in it.

I like rocker cots. They are a good size, and if baby takes a little while to settle you can give a little rock to help him drop off to sleep. Moses baskets are useful as you can take them with you when you go out and baby can still sleep flat, which is good for him. I don't like hammocks for young babies, as I like to be able to tuck baby securely into something firm.

It is not a good idea for babies to sleep in car seats for hours on end, as it is not good for their backs to be in the sitting up position for long periods of time. Neither should they have long sleeps in bouncy chairs or slings, as they do need to lie flat to sleep.

A large cot is good for baby when he is a bit bigger. Most babies, unless they are very large at birth, will sleep in a Moses basket or crib for about three months, or until they weigh about 12 lb or 5.5 kg. Then they will need to go into a big cot. Once they start putting their arms above their heads and touching the side of the cot they need to go into something bigger, as they can wake themselves up.

When you are buying the cot and pram it is a good idea to buy blankets and sheets at the same time. Cellular blankets wash and wear well. They are particularly good in the summer as the little holes mean they are breathable. I love a good shawl, although some are very warm, which is lovely if you have a winter baby but not so practical if baby is born in the summer. So, depending on the time of year you have your baby, buy accordingly. Duvets and quilts are not suitable for babies under one year old as baby can overheat. Your baby will not need a pillow. I do not recommend using a sleeping bag with very young babies under three months old.

A shopping list for sleeping

- Moses basket or crib and mattress
- Bedding for the Moses basket or crib: at least four fitted sheets, four cellular cotton blankets, four flat sheets (optional)
- Cot and mattress (optional at this age)
- Bedding for cot: four fitted sheets, four flat sheets, four large blankets (optional)
- Twelve to twenty-four muslins
- Two shawls for swaddling

- Room temperature gauge (optional)

- Baby monitor (optional)

Prams and buggies

It is also a good idea to look at prams or buggies when you are buying a cot. If you have room in your house or flat, a good comfortable pram is very useful. Make sure it has a supportive mattress and good springs and is easy to push and to fold up and put together again. If you have a car and will be taking baby out in it, then you need a pram or buggy that is easy to deal with. Some people buy the three-in-one variety. This is a car seat that fits on the buggy or on the top of the pram, which is useful if you are just popping out and don't want to disturb baby when he is sleeping. These "travel systems" are quite expensive but can be worth considering. Do ensure that any buggy you buy will fold down flat.

You will also need a car seat, as it is against the UK law to have a baby or child in the car without one. There are many to choose from, so try to look at as many as you can and choose whichever you think will be most suitable for you. Make sure it is properly fitted, otherwise it may not give as much protection as it should.

Some people like to take baby out in a sling. These are great if you are walking where you cannot take a pram or buggy, but a young baby shouldn't spend hours in a sling, as it is bad for their backs. Their little bones are so soft and they do need to lie flat to sleep.

A travel cot is a good investment, especially if you plan to go away often. It can also be used as a playpen when baby is a little bigger. Children can sleep in a travel cot for several years. Some are more comfortable than others, so do make sure that you buy one with a really good mattress. You may need to put a blanket under the mattress to bulk it up.

Playpens

A playpen is somewhere safe for you to put your baby, and he can go in it from a very young age. Playpens should be nice and solid: some have built in-floors. You can put a blanket down and put baby on top of this inside the playpen. Some mothers swaddle their babies and let them have short daytime naps on a blanket in the playpen. This works particularly well if you have another child running around.

Sleeping aids

Many babies suck their fingers or their thumbs. Very often baby will suck his thumb at a few days old. This can be a comfort for him when he wakes to feed and as he goes off to sleep. Sometimes he will suck his fists first and then his thumb.

The benefit of thumb-sucking rather than using a dummy is that baby can put his thumb in his mouth whenever he wants.

If you're not keen on thumb-sucking, when he is older you can let him do it at night but train him not to do it during the day.

Many babies will suck a muslin by the time they get to a few months old. You can tie one to the bars of his cot so that he can't cover his face with it, as this might be a suffocation risk.

Never leave a bottle of milk, juice, or water with a baby in his cot; he might choke on the bottle.

Dummies

Many people use a dummy or pacifier to help their baby to settle and to stop them crying. The main drawback of using a dummy is that you put the dummy in when baby is just dropping off to sleep but he spits it out, wakes up, and you are back to square one. You can spend all your time getting up and down to replace the dummy. And relying on a dummy can develop a habit that may be difficult and distressing to break. It is much better to teach baby to settle himself to sleep in the first place.

However, you can use a dummy to resettle baby in the night when you are teaching him to sleep through. If you have neighbours who can hear baby having a shout, then you may need to use a dummy to help him to settle. Take it away as soon as it has dropped out of his mouth and he is asleep.

Dummies can be a source of infection when dropped on the floor and put straight back into baby's mouth, so they need to be sterilized.

Musical toys, CDs, mobiles

There are some lovely musical toys such as teddies and other little animals that you can buy to go into baby's cot or hang on the end of it. You can turn these on when you settle him for sleep at night and he will gradually get used to their sounds as part of his night-time routine. To him the music will start to mean sleep.

You can also buy gentle, calming CDs that are specially produced for babies. These are also a good idea to use to help baby learn that it is bedtime. Babies very soon associate sounds with different times of the day.

Some people like to use mobiles over babies' cots but they aren't necessary for the first couple of months. However, they can be a good aid to entertain baby when he gets older.

"How to" guide

This part of the chapter will go through in detail how to settle your baby for sleep and how to begin to establish a good sleep routine.

Putting your baby down to sleep

How you put your baby down, and when, is important because a good routine will help a baby to settle well. Often new parents are not given guidance as to the best way of doing this.

Make sure baby has had a good feed, has brought up his wind, and has a clean nappy. Swaddle him, cuddle him into you, or put him on your shoulder and rub his back. Then he is ready to be tucked into his cot.

Swaddling

I am a great believer in swaddling as I have seen it work over and over again. Young babies sleep more deeply and for longer if they are swaddled. Unsettled babies often respond well to being swaddled.

You need to be careful you do not overheat your baby, so what you swaddle him in will depend on where you are in the world and what temperature baby's room is. In the UK, unless there is a heat wave, you can swaddle baby in a shawl or cellular blanket, then just pop a blanket over him which you tuck right down tight into the sides of the cot. It's better to have a cooler room and an extra blanket rather than fewer blankets and a room which is too warm, as it's preferable for baby to breathe in cool air than air which is too hot. Baby can wear a vest with a Babygro™ or sleepsuit over the top, before being swaddled in a shawl.

There are several ways to do the actual swaddling. You can either swaddle baby with both his arms down by his side, or with both arms up, or with one arm up and one arm down. Start with a shawl or cellular blanket and fold it over so that it is in a V shape. If you are swaddling baby with both arms down, lay him on his back in the centre of the V-shaped blanket with the blanket coming up to his neck so that it is not covering his face. Lay his hands down by his side, pull one side of the blanket over and tuck it under his body, then bring the other side of the blanket over his body and wrap round under his back. His head should be well up and the blanket should come under his chin.

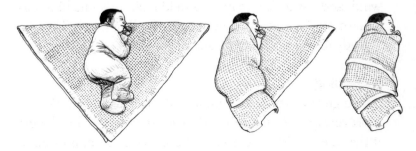

Swaddled like this he will find it difficult to get out of the blanket. This method really works if your baby is very tired and keeps throwing his arms up over his head and just cannot sleep. He will feel very secure once he is swaddled. Lay him on his back in his cot and tuck him in with one blanket over him.

If you are putting him on his side in his cot, lay him on the blanket on his side and lift both arms up so that he has his little hands at his face and can suck his fingers if he wants to. Bring the blanket round over his shoulder and tuck it in under his body, then bring the other side of the blanket over and tuck it right round him. He is then nice and secure and you can put him down in his cot on his side. A rolled-up blanket or towel at his back will keep him securely in position. Use another blanket to tuck him in.

You may wish to swaddle him with one arm in and one arm out. If so, use the same method as above but leave one arm tucked down by his side.

Sleep positions

Fashions come and go over the years regarding positions for sleeping. The current advice is to put baby down to sleep on his back. The FSID recommends that babies are best protected from cot death if they sleep on their backs until they are old enough to roll over easily and frequently, at around six months. They should not sleep on their tummies. However, babies may be more comfortable on their sides and usually sleep for longer in this position.

Once he is swaddled, your baby should be placed fairly well down the mattress, tucked in well, with the sheet or blanket coming up to his shoulders. His feet should nearly touch the bottom of the cot. Make sure he is tucked in firmly on each side and at the bottom so that he looks like a little roll in the cot. If you have him on his side, don't forget to roll up a small cotton cot blanket and place it behind his back. This gives support and prevents him rolling over. By the time he is around two months old he may well be moving onto his back anyway. Often you will put him down on his side but when you come to pick him up he has rolled onto his back. Don't put baby to sleep on his tummy. He will learn to roll onto his tummy when he is a few months old. If he will only settle lying on his tummy, pop him onto his back as soon as he is asleep.

How long should my baby sleep for?

Your aim is for your baby to sleep well in between feeds. If your baby was born at full term, after about one month he will start to be more wakeful after daytime feeds. If he was born very early, this may happen a little later. Baby should sleep for about an hour or so after the early morning feed (see the plan below). He should then sleep for two to three hours in the late morning, and again for about one to two hours in the afternoon. He should be in his cot again at about 7 p.m. After a late feed he should sleep for a longer period until he wakes in the night to be fed. After the night feed he should settle again and sleep until morning

Do remember that when your baby is newborn he is very likely to sleep a lot and may not have many wakeful times in the day. He will normally feed and then want to go straight back to sleep again, sometimes only having been up for about an hour at a time. This is perfectly normal. You may also find that at some feeds he is very sleepy and will only take a small feed. This is also fine as you will probably find that at the next feed he is hungrier and awake for longer.

For more information about feeding, have a look at my book, *The Baby Book: How to Enjoy Year One*.

Plan for the day

This is a guide to when you should encourage your baby to feed and sleep. It is only a guide: do be flexible if your times are different from these in the first few weeks and months as you may be feeding every three hours.

5 to 7 a.m. Your baby may wake up any time between 5 and 7 a.m. When baby wakes, feed him and change his nappy.

6 to 8 a.m. Your baby may have been awake for about an hour to an hour and a half, including his feed. Swaddle and put him back in his cot to sleep.

During his first two to three weeks he may only want to be up for about an hour, sometimes even less. If he just wants to feed and settle again, this is fine.

9:30 to 10:30 a.m. Your baby will probably wake up between 9:30 and 10:30 a.m. Top and tail him (wash his face, hands and bottom). Feed baby.

As baby gets older he will enjoy having a wakeful time after this feed (probably from three to four weeks onwards).

11 to 11:30 a.m. Swaddle and put baby down in his cot or pram to sleep.

Your baby should now sleep for about two or three hours. This is usually his main daytime sleep and he may continue to enjoy it at this time of the day for months to come.

2 to 2:30 p.m. If your baby hasn't woken on his own, wake him by 2:30 p.m.

Feed him and change his nappy.

3 to 3:30 p.m. Tuck baby down in his cot or pram to sleep

Your baby will normally sleep for about an hour and half, sometimes longer if he has been more wakeful in the morning. Wake him by 5:30 p.m. if he is still asleep.

5:30 to 6 p.m. Bath and feed baby.

7 to 7:30 p.m. After his feed is finished, swaddle baby and tuck him into his cot for the evening.

10 to 11 p.m. Wake and feed him if he doesn't wake of his own accord.

Change his nappy and settle him back in his cot after feeding. It's very important that this feed is a good one, as you want him to sleep for as long as possible through the night.

Night feed. This could be any time from 1 a.m. onwards, depending when you last fed him.

Feed him, making sure he has a full tummy, then tuck him down in his cot again. He may then sleep through until any time from 4 to 5 a.m. onwards. It's best not to wake a baby in the night to feed as you want to train him to have one long sleep in the twenty-four hours – and for this long sleep to be in the night. However, if a baby is jaundiced, underweight, or unwell then he may need to be woken to feed in the night.

Some parents don't wake their baby for a last feed at night (10 to 11 p.m.) as they want to go to bed earlier. This does work, as you just feed baby when he wakes. However, you will often find that this is no later than midnight and he still wakes again around 4 a.m.

As the months go on baby will gradually sleep for longer periods at night and eventually right through to the morning.

Baby's sleep cycle

A baby has a natural sleep cycle of about thirty to forty-five minutes, after which he enters a light sleep and may wake up. If he is used to being picked up at this stage instead of being left to resettle himself, then he will soon be in a habit of shouting and expecting to be picked up and fed or cuddled. This pattern is difficult to break once it is established.

It is important that baby is left to resettle himself when he wakes, or when he stirs on entering a light sleep phase. Once he has learned to do this he will be a much better sleeper.

How do I get my baby to settle?

Many parents want to know how they can get their baby to settle when they know he is tired and has been awake for long enough.

The first thing is to make sure that baby has had a good feed and won't take any more. Check that he has a clean nappy. Then swaddle him and put him on your shoulder, gently rubbing his back to make sure he hasn't got any wind.

Cuddle him, then lay him down in his cot. He doesn't need to fall asleep in your arms. Some newborn babies will go to sleep in your arms, but as they get older it is important to put them into their cots while they are still awake.

Tuck him in firmly and leave him to settle.

Don't go into him straight away if he doesn't settle. Many babies can take five to ten minutes to settle themselves.

If baby shouts and the shouting gets louder and louder and he is clearly not calming down, go in after ten minutes and pick him up. He may have wind, so put him on your shoulder and rub his back. If he is rooting and obviously hungry, put him back on the breast or offer him another 50 g (or 2 oz) of milk. Wind him and put him down in his cot again.

If his shouting decreases, leave him to settle himself.

If he still doesn't settle, rock his cot a little, but not for too long. This usually works with a new baby. However, it is important not to settle baby this way every time, as you risk ending up with a baby who will only settle by being rocked.

If your baby is a few weeks old you may need to leave him to have a shout for a bit longer. Sometimes he might take twenty minutes or so to settle. If you know that he is well fed and tired it is better to leave him to settle on his own.

However, if he still won't settle, doesn't have wind, and is not hungry, give him a cuddle and swaddle him again, putting him back into his cot either on his back or his side. Sometimes just changing position will help him to settle.

How not to settle baby

Don't resort to putting baby in the car and driving around the block, however tempting this is, as it can become a habit that will be difficult to break.

Avoid keeping him on the breast until he falls asleep and then putting him straight into his cot. This may seem an easy way to settle him when he is little, but by the time he is three to four months old you will find it impossible to settle him in any other way, and you will wish you had taught him to settle by himself. If he does fall asleep on the breast, take him off and gently wake him up so that he goes into his cot while he is awake.

Don't carry him around or rock him in your arms until he goes to sleep. This too is a habit that will be difficult to break.

So feeding baby to sleep or rocking him to sleep in your arms is very tempting but not a good idea. It can become exhausting and time-consuming if your baby will only go to sleep this way.

Never leave him in his cot with a bottle in his mouth, whatever his age.

How long will it take for baby to settle?

It is always difficult to let a new baby cry, especially if you are a first-time parent. It is a natural instinct to go to a crying baby and pick him up. As parents, we just want to cuddle him and make him better. This is perfectly normal and right. As he gets older it becomes easier to leave him to cry for a while.

If baby has fed and is well and healthy, then to leave him for ten minutes or so is quite acceptable. You may find this difficult, as it seems too long. If his shouting or crying is diminishing, if you can leave him, he will probably settle himself. Often he will have a real shout and you are just about to go in and pick him up when he stops. He may then start again after a few seconds or minutes. If he does, don't pick him up as he may well be settling himself. Have a look at him and if his eyes are closed and he looks sleepy, leave him. Lots of babies shout with their eyes tightly shut and when you look at them they appear to be shouting in their sleep. If this is the case, leave him for another few minutes.

For babies under three months old, there isn't really a set length of time to leave them to cry. If you find it too distressing to listen to baby shout, go somewhere where you can't hear him, or turn the radio on and try counting to 200 as this may help you to deal with it. You may well find that he stops by himself.

Should I wake my baby to feed him?

I am a great believer in waking baby up to feed during the day and up until the 10 to 11 p.m. feed. You may find that this last evening feed is a "dream feed": baby has his eyes closed the whole time he feeds and appears not to wake up at all. This is perfectly OK. Just wind him and change him as usual when he has finished and tuck him back down in his cot.

Then don't wake him during the night. You want him to start learning to sleep for a longer stretch, and you want this stretch to be at night. If you feed him regularly every three to four hours during the day you will very soon find that he will automatically sleep for a long stretch at some stage during the night.

During the day, if you are feeding him three hourly, count three hours from the beginning of that feed. If he is feeding four hourly, then it is four hours from the beginning of the last feed. If you do this, baby will soon get into a habit of sleeping till his next feed. It is interesting how quickly their little body clocks get tuned into sleep and feed times. Within a few weeks you may find baby waking on the dot of three or four hours to feed.

If baby wakes up before a feed is due, be flexible with him. If he is still only a few days or weeks old, don't make him wait; if he is hungry, then feed him. If you are trying to move him on to the next feed you can always take him for a walk in the pram as he may settle again for another half an hour.

Troubleshooting guide

If your baby is healthy there is no reason why he should not sleep. It is the natural thing for a baby to do. However, some babies need more help with sleeping than others, and babies can get into bad sleeping habits very quickly. When you know what to do, and are consistent and persevere, you can build good sleeping habits that will benefit not only your baby but the entire family.

What do I do if my baby won't sleep?

Sometimes a baby will feed well but just not settle afterwards. This often happens in the night when he is about two to four weeks old.

First, make sure he doesn't have any wind. Pick him up, put him on your shoulder, and rub his back firmly. If he has wind he will burp. If not, he may need a top-up feed, so put him back on the breast. It may only be comfort sucking, but often that will settle him. Only change his nappy again if it is dirty. Wind him, then tuck him down in his cot again. You may need to rock the cot a little, but he will usually settle.

If you don't think you have any more milk and he is hungry, give some expressed breast milk in a bottle, or offer him one to two ounces (25–50 g) of formula. This may just be what he needs to settle him.

Baby may not be settling because he is overtired. This could be because he was awake for a while before his feed. Again put baby back on the breast and let him feed for five minutes or so, wind him, then tuck him firmly down in his cot. Even if baby is overtired this extra little top-up should encourage him to settle down.

Sometimes you can find that a baby just won't settle at all in between two feeds and whatever you do he will sleep for perhaps five to ten minutes and then be on the go again. This is exhausting not only for you but for baby too. If this happens I would cuddle him into you to try and calm him down if it is night-time, and then give him a good feed and see if this will settle him.

If it is daytime I would put him in the pram or buggy and take him out for a walk, or get a friend or your partner to take him out. Usually this will send baby off to sleep but you may find when you stop pushing the pram he wakes straight away.

By this time it is probably nearly time for the next feed so I would give him a good feed (even if it is not quite feed time), change his nappy, and tuck him into his cot. If his tummy is full he should then settle and have a good sleep for a few hours.

Reasons for crying and failing to sleep

Babies have different cries, and when you are a new parent it is often difficult to know what each cry means. Don't worry as you will soon get to know which is which.

Hunger

Hunger is a main cause of crying. Baby's "hungry" cry often sounds quite desperate. He will often suck his fists and turn his head from side to side. You will not be able to pacify a hungry baby, and he will not settle even if you tuck him down in his cot. If you hold him in your arms he will turn his head into your arm and start sucking. As soon as you put him on the breast or give him the bottle he will feed very well and keep going until he comes off to be winded.

However, babies will often show hunger signs when they are tired, which can be misleading when you are a new parent. So if in doubt, offer baby more feed. If he is not hungry he may fall asleep on the breast, or push the teat or nipple out and make a face at you. Then you know he doesn't need any more, so tuck him up in his cot to sleep.

Tiredness

A tired cry sounds less desperate. Again, he will probably suck his fingers and turn his head from side to side. He will look miserable, and may be pale and wide-eyed. Always take a note of the time when he wakes or you wake him to feed. If baby has been up for longer than one and a half hours he needs to be put down in his cot. New babies can get tired from being over-handled and passed around from person to person, so do watch out for this.

Wind

Lots of parents get very anxious about whether their baby has wind or not, and will spend a long time trying to get him to burp when he doesn't need to. If your baby has got wind he will cry out and bring his little legs up. He will be obviously uncomfortable or in pain.

As a rule, breast fed babies don't have as much wind as bottle-fed babies. However, a breast fed baby still needs winding, especially if you have a lot of milk and a fast let down. Put baby on your shoulder and rub his back firmly, or sit him up on your knee with one hand on his tummy and your other hand on his back and give a good firm rub. You should find he does a big burp. Sometimes, carrying him up and down stairs moves trapped wind. Laying him down on his back, then sitting him upright also works, as does laying him on his tummy on your lap and rubbing his back.

Colic or evening wakefulness

Many parents are frightened that their baby has or will have colic. However, if your baby is settled after feeds during the day and in the night but not after the early evening feed, this is not colic but just evening wakefulness. Many babies are wakeful at this time of the day, but they will grow out of this by the time they are around twelve weeks old. It may not happen every evening, and for no apparent reason some evenings baby may settle perfectly well.

Colic is tummy pain, and a colicky baby will bring his knees up to his tummy and have a good shout. The best way to ease his pain is to put him on your shoulder and rub his back. When baby is held fairly upright this will help his tummy ache. Often babies who are fed little and often, or demand fed, will get colic or tummy ache as their tummies are never very full.

Some parents will just feed their grumpy baby on and off all evening. I'm not keen on this idea as you are continually up and down to baby and don't get any time together without baby. Some parents carry their babies around all the time but this just makes for an overtired baby who, when you come to feed him next, will not take a full feed but fall asleep on the breast or bottle. You then find you are up again in a few hours time feeding again.

As I have already said, if baby doesn't settle, try feeding him once again and then put him down in his cot. If he doesn't settle, or only settles on and off all evening, give him his next feed early, maybe even by 9:45 p.m. You will probably find he will sleep well after this feed and for most of the night too.

Too hot or too cold

If a baby has been sleeping well at night and wakes for no apparent reason, check he is not cold. Check his body temperature by feeling the back of his neck, and check the temperature in the room. He may need another blanket or a heater in his bedroom.

Baby will also wake if he is too hot. Again check the temperature of the back of his neck. If he is too hot this will feel very warm to the touch and his little face will be flushed. His hands will feel hot, and when you get him out of his cot his body will be sweaty. Check the heating in his room, and adjust accordingly.

Baby can get too hot when he is all wrapped up for being outside and you take him into a hot shop. Peel his blankets off while you are in the shop and then tuck him in again when you go outside.

Older babies can overheat under rain covers on buggies when the sun comes out, or when you go into a shop. Always undo the rain cover when the temperature rises.

Reflux

Reflux (also known as gastro-reflux) can be a very distressing complaint for both baby and parents, as you usually find you have a very uncomfortable and unsettled little one. Don't despair, and take comfort that this will pass.

Reflux is what happens when the sphincter muscle at the top of baby's stomach has not completely developed and is weaker than usual, allowing milk to come up again, either as projectile vomit, or as normal vomiting. Baby may start showing signs of this from about four weeks old. You will notice that he is beginning to be more unsettled after feeds and may be sick either after his feed or when you have put him down in his cot. Sometimes babies have "silent reflux": they are hardly sick at all but are obviously very uncomfortable at feed time. Babies with reflux will pull off the breast or bottle and clearly be uncomfortable.

If you think your baby has reflux, get in touch with your GP, who may prescribe an antacid for baby and a thicker feed if you are bottle-feeding.

Dairy intolerance

It seems that more and more babies and children are being diagnosed with milk intolerance of some sort or other. These intolerances can bring about nasty symptoms and it is often some time before a diagnosis is given. Babies can show signs of reflux and vomiting; they may fail to gain weight, cry a lot, and be miserable. They may also have bowel problems such as diarrhoea. If you are concerned, you need to speak to your GP, who will advise you on feeding and any medication that may be needed.

Nappy rash

Young babies sometimes get nappy rash, which can make them very uncomfortable and restless if it is not treated. Use a good barrier cream and if it doesn't heal up then see your GP or health visitor about it.

Changing time zones

You may travel with your new baby to a different time zone and wonder how your little one will manage with sleeping and feeding. The best solution is to let him sleep and feed when he needs to on the journey. If you are flying he will need plenty of fluids. When you reach your destination, if he has been awake a long time, feed him and tuck him down to sleep. Make sure you feed him every three to four hours and then let him sleep longer in the night if he will do so. I am always amazed at how quickly babies and young children adapt to a new time zone – much more quickly than we do!

Twins

It's particularly important that you have a routine with twins, otherwise you end up feeding them at different times and they sleep at different times and you never have any time for yourself. So it is vital that twins sleep and feed at the same time as each other. You can use the feed timing plan and all the sleep advice above for twins, just as you would for a single baby. Twins may settle and sleep better if they are not sharing one cot, but this is a matter of preference, especially with newborn babies. If you find that one twin is waking in the night while the other is sleeping through, it is perfectly all right to put them in separate rooms or separate cots so that they don't disturb each other. Once they are both sleeping through the night you can put them back together again.

Case studies

Jacqui

Daniel was eight weeks old when we contacted you. He had absolutely no routine. His discomfort during feeding over the previous six weeks had meant that he would feed only little and often, and we never knew where we were as a result. We started off by suspecting that he had reflux, but after several visits to doctors and a consultant we narrowed the problem down to milk intolerance. I never really knew if his disrupted sleep pattern was due to overtiredness, or hunger, or both. Neither Daniel nor I had been getting much sleep during the night as he would feed every two hours. He would sleep in his basket in the kitchen during the day, until 11 to 12 p.m., when I would take him into my bedroom. He was also getting into a difficult situation in relying on a dummy to settle, which meant that I was continually putting it back in his mouth during the night when it had fallen out.

I was feeling constantly stressed due to lack of sleep and really didn't know what to do for the best. I was arguing more with my partner and I was worried about the impact all this was having on our older child, Florence. Because of Daniel's erratic feeding and sleeping pattern I felt trapped in the house and unable to take Florence out as much as I would have liked.

You advised us to implement a routine with feeding times at 6 to 7 a.m., 10 to 11 a.m., 2 to 3 p.m., and a split feed on either side of bath time. You also helped us not to pick Daniel up immediately, but to let him learn to settle himself (which I know he can do).

We moved him to his bedroom for most of his naps and sleep. No more sleeping in the kitchen! For his midday sleep, you advised us to use the pram and go for a walk to help get him into a good sleeping pattern. You also recommended that we lose the dummy.

You suggested that we drop the dream feed – we know he is able to last for longer, so why wake him before he is ready for a big feed? By leaving him to wake naturally at about 1 a.m., we found that he would take a large feed, which took him through to 6 or 7 a.m.

We found your advice relatively easy to follow, although his midday sleep proved difficult for a while. He wouldn't settle for the entire time, and sometimes we found it difficult to let him cry. A split feed at bath time worked well. Daniel is now settling well to sleep at 6:30 p.m. – so we have our evenings back. We fell into a routine fairly quickly and found that Daniel would settle better at bedtime – this was a major breakthrough. Our baby is more settled and much more content – and as a result, so am I!

Nicola

Henry was about five weeks old when I first got in touch with you. I was beginning to feel desperate, as Henry wasn't sleeping at all well. He would often only achieve a total of forty-five minutes sleep throughout the entire day. He seemed to be constantly hungry, and with feeds taking forty to fifty minutes each it was almost time for the next feed once I had fed him, changed his nappy, and tried to get him to sleep. The whole household was exhausted and frustrated as we couldn't work out what we were doing wrong.

We were in a vicious circle. I was so determined to feed on demand that I'd forgotten that crying could also be due to tiredness. It seems so obvious now, but I was in a bit of a newborn/new parent daze. Poor Henry was too tired to feed properly and too hungry to sleep properly. You suggested I top him up with some formula to make his tummy really full and cosy so that he would start sleeping longer and the cycle would be broken. It worked a treat and I soon established a three-hour schedule. Henry became a much more content little boy and I began to feel a lot more confident as a parent.

I also used your great techniques for making Henry feel secure, cosy, and able to sleep. Swaddling him properly in a cotton cellular blanket has proved invaluable.

Polly

I contacted Rachel when my first child, Rose, was four and a half weeks old and again when my second child, Flora, was nearly six weeks old.

I quickly got Rose into a "Waddilove" routine, but if she had a full feed at 6:30 p.m. she wouldn't want much milk at 10:30 p.m. This meant she would wake up at about 2 a.m. for a feed. But if I didn't feed her much at 6:30 p.m. she would cry and cry until her 10:30 p.m. feed, then take a full feed and sleep for longer. The problem was the crying between 7 and 10 p.m., as she was clearly hungry. It was very stressful for everyone.

You advised me to try to give Rose a full feed at 6:30 p.m.

and feed her again later on, at perhaps 11:30 p.m., when she would be hungrier. This worked brilliantly! She slept from 11 p.m. until 7:30 a.m. from when she was about nine weeks old.

Flora had massive "witching hour" issues from 5 p.m. until bedtime. However, if we didn't let her have a shout she would be wakeful from 7 until 10 p.m., which we had already combated in the earlier weeks. Her shouting became an issue for everyone as she was all over the place when she cried – sweaty, red-faced and completely beside herself. This was extremely stressful.

You suggested I give Flora a little feed at about 5 p.m. This worked well, but she still had a shout from about 6:15 p.m. To be honest, I think she was just tired, as she does a similar thing now, at nearly six months old. As you pointed out, she needed to have her wakeful time at some point during the day, and that was her time.

Both your sets of advice were very easy to implement and worked perfectly. With Rose it worked almost immediately. Although with Flora it took a bit longer, I think that may have been due to her personality!

With each child, I underestimated the impact that lack of sleep has on the family. It makes even the strongest person crumble. Getting these sleep issues sorted out meant that we could enjoy each of our new additions rather than see them through a haze of tiredness. I have followed your routines and now have three children who all sleep perfectly, still have a sleep during the day, and I think are happier for it. Many friends I look at are exasperated by their children and I think, these little ones are just tired, no wonder they are kicking off. People might scoff at routine, but it makes for a much happier family life.

Sleep solutions:
three to six months

By the time your baby is three months old you may well be feeling more settled and be in a good routine. You will have spent time getting to know this little person and his needs and wants. Most parents feel very much more relaxed with their three-month-old baby: he can sit in his chair, he will enjoy having more wakeful times in the day, and will interact much more with you. It is always lovely when baby smiles and chuckles when you walk into the room. Somehow it makes all those broken nights seem worthwhile! However, you may still be having broken nights and baby's daytime sleep pattern may be all over the place. Many parents feel that three months is a good time to start sleep training. They feel more confident about leaving their baby to have a shout and settle on his own.

How much sleep should my baby have?

Your baby should be having about sixteen hours' sleep in twenty-four hours. You may find that from about four months to six months he will start to sleep through the night, from 7 p.m. to about 7 a.m., but many babies don't do this, for all sorts of reasons. If your baby isn't sleeping through, don't worry, it's not too late to teach him.

By the time he is six months old, baby should be sleeping for about twelve hours at night and having three naps during the day. If you are still feeding him in the night, he will sleep less. He should have a nap for about one hour in the early morning, another sleep about two hours later, and his third nap for about an hour in the afternoon.

As with a newborn, a baby aged three to six months has a natural sleep cycle of about thirty to forty-five minutes. Then he will enter a light sleep and may wake up. If he has always been picked up at this stage instead of being left to resettle himself, he will soon be in a habit of shouting and expecting to be picked up, fed, or cuddled. This is a difficult pattern to break. It is important that baby is left to resettle himself when he wakes or stirs. This will make him a much better sleeper.

How to settle a three- to six-month-old baby

If you have had trouble settling your baby from the early days and maybe not had any sort of routine, you will probably want to get this sorted out sooner rather than later. It is a good idea to have a method, and stick to it as much as you can without it becoming prescriptive and making you more anxious than before.

First, make sure baby has a good full tummy and a clean nappy. You may not be swaddling him during these next three months, so wrap him in a blanket or shawl, underneath his arms, or put him in his Grobag. Give him a cuddle and tuck him in his cot or pram, talking to him as you do this. Stroke his head and tell him that you love him, then leave the room. If he is very wound up and overtired, spend more time cuddling him and sitting in the chair in his room with the lights down and rocking him on your lap. Sometimes singing softly in a baby's ear can calm him down ready for sleep. When you have done this, lay him in his cot, tuck him in, kiss good night, and leave the room.

During the day the trick is to get him to sleep until his next feed time. Then feed him, change him, and let him have a play time. This is either a kick on his baby gym or on his changing mat, or sitting in his little chair. After this he will be ready for his nap and will sleep through to the next feed. This is really what you are aiming for.

Where should my baby sleep?

I recommend that baby sleeps in his own room by the time he is three months old, particularly if you are trying to sleep train him. In my experience it is almost impossible to train a baby to sleep when he is in the same room as you. His crying can really get to you and the need to pick him up for a bit of peace and quiet can be overwhelming.

If baby does need to share your bedroom because of a lack of space where you live, see if you can borrow a screen, or get an old one in a sale. That will help to screen you off from each other. You may need to use a dummy to help cut the noise down.

If your baby has been ill or was very premature you may want to keep him in the same room as you for a while longer.

His cot or my bed?

If your baby weighs over 12 lb or 5.5 kg he will probably need to go into a big cot or a cot bed. He may be waking himself up by touching the sides or ends of a Moses basket or crib, and he will sleep better in the big cot. Some people buy a cot bed that will last for several years. These are a good idea and provide plenty of space for a growing baby.

It is unwise to let baby sleep in your bed. As he gets bigger and starts rolling about, he might fall off. There is also a risk of you rolling over and suffocating him. Baby needs to go in his own cot and get used to sleeping on his own. He will sleep much better there and will grow to love his own cot and bed as time goes on.

Some people worry that their baby will suffer from separation anxiety if they put him in his own cot and room. However, babies who have their own cots and rooms or share with siblings don't generally suffer from separation anxiety. If they do, there are usually other underlying family problems.

Sleeping during the day

It is good if baby can sleep somewhere different in the day. You may have a pram or buggy in which he will be comfortable. By the time he is four to six months old it is a good idea to strap him into his pram, as he will become more active during these three months. However, he can still go in his cot for daytime naps and probably will do so more as he gets older. It is not a good idea to put baby in your bed to sleep during the day, for the same reasons as given above.

Many of baby's daytime naps may be taken on the move, but do try and tuck him in his cot particularly after his 6 to 7 a.m. feed. He will need a good sleep, if possible quietly in his cot away from the rest of the family, before his 10 to 11 a.m. feed. Newborn babies will sleep through noise but by the time they are three months old they will wake up very easily so they need to sleep somewhere quiet.

If you have a garden it is a lovely idea for baby to sleep in his pram outside. Make sure it is safe and that no one can take him. Do put a cat/insect net over the pram, and keep it out of direct sunlight. Keep watch for cats, squirrels, and foxes as in some areas they can be quite tame and rather bold.

Many babies will sleep in the car. This is helpful if you have a toddler at nursery or school age children and you are doing school runs. Often a baby who has been used to this from the beginning will nap quite well on the move but may not settle or sleep as well when he is in his cot at home. Do try and put him to sleep in his cot whenever you can.

Nearly all babies sleep well when being pushed out for walks, whether in a buggy or a pram.

Sleep positions
By the time baby is three months old he will most likely be sleeping on his back and you may well have him in a Grobag. Some babies will still sleep swaddled on their sides with a rolled up blanket or shawl behind them. If your baby is still doing this, it is absolutely fine and you can continue for as long as he is comfortable and sleeping well. You will probably find that he will roll onto his back while he sleeps.

A lot of babies will settle better on their tummies by this age. Parents often ask me about the safety aspect of this. If baby will only settle on his tummy, turn him over onto his back once he is asleep. As baby gets older he will usually prefer to go to sleep on his tummy. When you settle him in his cot make sure his feet nearly touch the end and tuck him in with blankets if he isn't wearing a Grobag. If he is cosy in a Grobag he probably won't need a blanket as well.

Should I wake my baby to feed?

It is important that you don't let your baby sleep for hours on end in the day without feeding him. Now that he is older you will find that he is more wakeful in the day and you are unlikely to have this problem. You will probably be feeding him every three to four hours during the day. If this has not happened, gradually train him to go longer between feeds so that you have a pattern of four hours between feeds.

Sleep aids

Many babies suck their thumbs from an early age. Some parents fear that the habit will go on until the child is almost grown up. Parents can also be concerned that their child will have problems with sore thumbs and his front teeth sticking out. However, it is impossible to stop a baby from sucking his thumb at night, as he will pop it into his mouth automatically. Thumb-sucking can also help him to settle. Children generally grow out of the habit quite naturally.

Dummies

Many people use dummies as a way to have some peace and quiet and to settle their babies. If you have used one since baby was born you could wean him off it during these three months before he gets too hooked on it. This is really a matter of individual choice, but I think the earlier baby is weaned off a dummy the better. When he gets older and can stand up in his cot and lose his dummy over the side, weaning can be much harder.

So, if you want to wean baby off a dummy now, use it to settle him if he is reliant on it, but don't put it back in his mouth if he wakes for it. Introduce a cuddly toy or blanket that he can get used to instead. If you can't face taking the dummy away because you are afraid of the fuss he will make, wait till he is older and you can explain that it is going in the bin or to a new baby. Make sure that an older baby doesn't walk around with a dummy in his mouth all day. It is not good for his teeth or his speech development to be chewing on one all the time.

Mobiles

Using a mobile over the cot to help baby settle to sleep tends to be a bit hit and miss: it works some times and not others. It is much better for your baby to learn to sleep without it. A mobile can overstimulate a baby who is already tired and needs to settle down, particularly in the evenings. However, it is a fun aid to have over the cot when baby is having a kick and a wakeful time during the day.

Cuddly toys, blankets and muslins

From about the age of three months a baby will start to get attached to a cuddly toy or blanket, so this is a good age to introduce one. You may have already been putting one in his cot and that is fine. There are some lovely soft, small cuddly bunnies that children seem to love and keep for years. You could tie a muslin cloth to the side of the bars of his cot, as some babies love their muslins.

It is reassuring for baby to have something that he associates with sleep and settling down in his cot. Remember to have a second cuddly so that if you lose one or it needs to go in the wash, you have a spare.

Musical toys

There are attractive lovely little musical toys that can be hung on the end of baby's cot or placed at the end of the cot. Some are teddies with a musical box inside, some are little animals that play lullaby tunes. They play a soothing tune that baby will recognize as part of going in his cot for sleeps.

Feeding bottles

Never leave a bottle of juice or milk to settle baby in his cot. It is not a good habit to get into as the milk or juice may damage his first teeth if he is left sucking until the bottle falls out of his mouth. And there is a danger of baby choking on the bottle, whatever it contains.

Sleep plan for three to six months

6 to 7 a.m. Your baby will probably wake any time between 6 and 7 a.m. Feed him when he wakes.

If he hasn't woken by 7:30 a.m., wake him to feed.

7:30 to 8:30 a.m. Your baby will be awake for about an hour and a half, including his feed. This time may be longer as he nears six months of age.

If he wakes at 6 a.m. tuck him back in his cot by 7:30 to 8 a.m.

If he wakes at 7 a.m. he should be back in his cot by 8 to 8:30 a.m.

Your baby will probably sleep for up to an hour and a half. If it's two hours, it doesn't matter.

10 to 11 a.m. Wake your baby by 10:30 a.m. if he hasn't woken up by himself (he may wake any time from 9:30 a.m.).

Top and tail baby, and feed him.

He will probably enjoy a wakeful time for about an hour and a half.

11:30 a.m. to 12 noon. Tuck baby down in his pram or cot for a sleep.

Baby should sleep for one and a half to two hours.

2 to 3 p.m. Wake baby by 2:30 p.m. if he hasn't woken by himself.

Feed him, change his nappy, and have a play time.

3:30 to 4 p.m. Put baby in his pram or cot to sleep. This sleep will usually be shorter, up to about an hour.

Make sure baby is up by 5:30 p.m. or it can be difficult to settle him for the night at 7 p.m.

By the time your baby is four to six months old, you may be giving him some solids at teatime, around 5 p.m. If you are, just slot this in after his afternoon nap and before bath time.

5:30 to 6 p.m. Bath time.

6 to 6:45 p.m. Bedtime feed.

Try to do this feed in his bedroom or somewhere quiet to help him to get ready to settle down for the night.

7 to 7:30 p.m. Settle baby in his cot for the night.

10 to 11 p.m. (optional)

Wake baby for his dream feed if he still needs one.

Change his nappy and settle him straight back into his cot.

Again it's a good idea to keep this feed quiet with the lights low, so he doesn't get overstimulated.

You may not be waking baby for a dream feed as you may prefer to go to bed yourself and sleep till he wakes in the night. This is fine, and you will gradually find over the months that baby will sleep longer until he is sleeping for twelve hours from 7 p.m. to 7 a.m.

Troubleshooting guide

You may well have found that your baby slept well in the first few weeks of life and was very settled but now is not settling as well and wakes early for feeds. If this is the case, the first question to ask is, "Is he having enough to drink?" The main reason for babies not settling or waking early for feeds is that they are hungry, so this does need to be looked at first.

The current advice is not to start giving your baby solids until he is six months old. For most babies this is not early enough. Fashions do change, but when baby weighs around 14 to 15 lb (6.35 to 6.8 kg), and is hungry, you should start him on some solid food. So, if your baby is not sleeping after having previously been settled, or if he is waking earlier and earlier in the morning, he probably needs some solid food in his tummy. For more information about introducing solids, have a look at my book, *The Baby Book: How to Enjoy Year One* and Annabel Carmel's *New Complete Baby and Toddler Meal Planner*.

What do you do if baby isn't hungry but still won't settle himself? Many babies find it hard to self settle if they are used to being picked up as soon as they cry. Other babies may have got used to falling asleep at the breast, or being rocked to sleep in a parent's arms, or being taken out for a drive to help them settle. It is harder to teach them to settle themselves as they get older, but it's not impossible, so don't despair if this is your problem. It is important to remember that you won't be able to train your baby overnight: you need to give yourselves at least a week, maybe two.

Try to follow the feeding and sleeping routine above, particularly if you have been demand feeding and have no structure to your day. When you have fed baby and you know he is full, he should have a wakeful time after his daytime feeds. When he has been up for about one and a half to two hours he will be getting grumpy and this is the time to tuck him down in his cot or pram. You probably won't be swaddling him anymore as he may be too big for this and kicks or wriggles out of the blanket.

If he has a shout and doesn't stop, but shouts more loudly and gets very worked up, pick him up. Check for wind: if he burps, cuddle him on your shoulder for a minute, then tuck him back in his cot and leave him. He may be rooting and pushing his fists in his mouth. If so, he is probably still hungry, so top him up with five minutes on the breast or offer him another ounce (25 g) or so of formula. Then tuck him back down. You may need to both wind and feed him.

After tucking baby into his cot it is fine to leave him for ten to fifteen minutes to settle on his own. It is normal for some babies to cry and shout when they are settling themselves after a feed. However, if he continues shouting and won't settle, you may want to start using the controlled crying method I explain later in this chapter.

If baby is not hungry, and you know he can settle himself, there may be other reasons why he is not settling.

Colic and evening wakefulness

Colic is trapped wind which causes baby pain or discomfort. He will bring his knees up, shout, and clearly be uncomfortable. Usually a baby who has this sort of tummy ache is happier when you put him on your shoulder, rub his back, and walk around with him. You can usually tuck baby down in his cot after a while, once the wind has passed. In my experience, babies who are fed regularly and well tend not to suffer with many bouts of colic.

There are various medications that you can give before baby feeds to help alleviate colic. (Infacol is probably the most widely used.) In all honestly I am not sure how effective they are but they can make mum feel better as she has tried something to soothe baby.

If your baby is very good and settled after every feed during the day and night but is unsettled in the early evening and stays awake until his last feed, this is not colic. Baby is just having a wakeful time and airing his lungs. Unfortunately it is always at the time of day when you want to settle down for the evening. If your three-month-old baby is still doing evening shouting, I promise you it won't go on for much longer.

Reflux

Reflux is what happens when the sphincter muscle at the top of baby's stomach is not properly formed. It is a nasty complaint that causes real discomfort and pain. It usually starts when baby is about five weeks old and can continue in severe cases until he is nearly a year. More usually it rights itself during baby's third to sixth month as he grows and develops and starts eating solid food.

Dairy intolerance

Dairy milk intolerance and lactose intolerance are unpleasant complaints which can show the same sort of signs as reflux. Baby will show signs of being very uncomfortable after a feed, usually a few weeks after birth. It can be difficult to diagnose and it is important that you get medical advice from your GP.

Teething

Baby will start teething from the age of about four months onwards and may well wake in the night with pain. The best thing to do is use teething granules and Calpol to ease his pain. You may find his sleep pattern goes out of schedule and you are up and down in the night for a little while. It is important to keep his bedtime routine normal and not get him up any more than is necessary during the night. As soon as he has settled down, be firm with him if he wakes in the night again. However, teething can sometimes undo good sleeping habits for a while.

Illness

Illness of any kind can keep a baby awake at night. If your baby is unwell, he needs to be comforted and given the correct medication. You should also give him a drink of either milk or water, especially if he has a raised temperature. If he has an upset tummy with sickness and diarrhoea, he will probably need diluted milk or no milk at all for a while, just boiled water. Do check with your GP if your baby is ill; this can provide important reassurance for you too.

Some babies are particularly susceptible to ear infections. These can flare up quickly, be very painful and keep a baby awake at night. Signs of an ear infection are usually a red ear, baby rubbing his ear, and a raised temperature. You will need to see your GP, who may prescribe antibiotics. Do give Calpol or Nurofen to ease baby's pain.

Babies can develop bronchiolitis at any age from newborn until about eighteen months. In the UK it often occurs between the months of October and March. It is an upper and lower respiratory infection affecting the breathing tubes that run from the nose to the lungs. This can produce a nasty cough, breathlessness, difficulty in feeding, rapid, laboured breathing, and a change of skin colour. You need to get medical attention quickly if this happens to your baby.

Croup is another nasty complaint and can be muddled with bronchiolitis as the cough is very similar. Do go and see your GP if you are concerned.

Nappy rash

Babies can develop nappy rash very quickly, often when they are teething. Use a good barrier cream, and if the rash doesn't clear up consult your GP or health visitor.

How do I know when my baby is tired?

Many parents ask how they can tell when their baby is tired and ready to settle to sleep. Always keep an eye on the time so that you know when you woke baby or he woke for a feed. After he has been awake for about one and a half to two hours he may become grumpy and will be ready to settle to sleep again. When babies get overtired it is much more difficult for them to settle, so try not to let this happen.

Baby will often show you that he is sleepy by yawning, turning his head from side to side, and rubbing his eyes.

Many babies will turn pale and wide-eyed and look miserable. If you hold baby in your arms and rock him he may close his eyes and start to go to sleep. If this happens you should tuck him down at once; if he actually goes to sleep in your arms he will probably wake up as soon as you lay him in his cot.

Establishing good bedtime and morning routines

It is important to establish a good bedtime routine each day if possible. Obviously there are some days when you will be out and about, but a good bedtime routine helps baby to feel secure. If baby isn't settling well, try starting bath time and bedtime a little earlier. You will be less likely to feel stressed and you will be able to spend a little more time with baby, helping him to wind down and having cuddles before putting him in his cot.

Try to make sure there are no sudden noises nearby when baby is settling. You don't need to ensure silence in the house, as it is useful if he learns to go to sleep with general noises like the telephones ringing, traffic outside, and family life going on in other rooms.

It is important not to stimulate baby just before bedtime, as he needs some winding down time, particularly if he is finding it difficult to settle. Resist the temptation to jump him up into the air or to tickle him just before he goes to bed. Have fun and games in the daytime instead.

Always try to put baby in his cot when he is still awake. Obviously sometimes he may be very tired and already starting to fall asleep, but in general make sure that he goes into his cot awake.

Keep a routine of good nap times in the day, at the same time, if you possibly can. It is a myth that if baby doesn't sleep in the day he will sleep better at night; it just doesn't work like that. The better baby sleeps in the day, the more he will sleep at night.

How not to settle your three- to six-month-old

- Don't rock baby to sleep in your arms.
- Don't let him feed until he goes to sleep and then put him in his cot.
- Don't push him round in his pram until he goes to sleep.
- Don't take him for a drive in the car to settle him.
- Don't let him get overtired, as this will make him difficult to settle.
- Don't go immediately to baby when he cries.
- Don't sit with him until he goes to sleep.
- Don't lie on the floor by his cot while he goes to sleep.
- Don't leave a bottle in his mouth or in his cot.

How long should it take my baby to settle?

All babies are different and some settle very quickly while others can take longer. You may well find that if you have several children they have all had slightly different sleeping patterns. Generally, however, a baby between the ages of three and six months should settle to sleep within fifteen minutes of being put in his cot. You may find that at some times of the day he always settles more quickly than at others. Don't worry if this happens: it is normal behaviour.

What if my baby just won't sleep?

Some babies do sleep better than others and some need more training. A parent who is a light sleeper may have a child who is similar. However, all babies can be trained to sleep if you know what to do, and you are consistent and persevere. Over all the years I have been helping with sleep training I have never known a baby or child who has not been trainable. As long as a baby is fit and healthy he can be trained to sleep.

How to cope with a crying baby

All parents find that having a shouting baby who will not settle is exhausting and emotionally draining. There are many things that worry parents about a baby crying: whether he will be psychologically damaged, whether he will remember being left to cry when he wakes in the morning, or whether he will wake the other children in the family. Leaving a well-fed, healthy, well-loved, and well cared-for baby to cry for a limited time while he settles himself to sleep is altogether different from leaving a hungry, wet baby alone for hours. The latter is abuse and is never right.

You need to survive and get through the disturbance of a crying baby. If he shouts a lot during the day it is easier to deal with than when he shouts at night. During the day you can shut the door, go and do something else, and try not to listen. Turn the baby monitor down or off so that you don't hear every little squeak and sound baby makes. If you can, go into the garden and count to 200. Sit down and listen to some soothing music or make a cake if you like baking. As soon as baby goes to sleep, put your feet up for half an hour or so if you can.

If it is all getting too much for you and you're not coping, ask for help. Perhaps a friend or relation could come in and give you company and support, or enable you to go out and do something that you want to do for yourself. It is important to have a break from the baby if you are feeling very tense and stressed. If you are finding it all too difficult to cope with, then consult your GP.

At night it is important that baby sleeps in his own room, as it is impossible to sleep train him if his cot is beside your bed. If you only have one bedroom you might consider moving out yourself, perhaps sleeping on a mattress in another room until baby is sleeping better. As during the day, turn the baby monitor down so that you can't hear every little noise he makes during the night.

Remember that by teaching baby to sleep, you are doing him a huge favour. You are showing him a great deal of love by setting helpful boundaries for him. In parenting terms, this is just the beginning. Teaching your baby to sleep can be one of the easiest things to do compared to some of the other issues you will face as he grows up.

If you have neighbours nearby who can hear your baby having a shout, do go and talk to them. Explain that you are sleep training him and they will understand what is going on when they hear him crying. Most people are very sympathetic and will understand what you are doing.

Sleep training methods

The two methods I use are controlled crying and "shout it out" or cold turkey.

A three-month-old baby is not too young for the controlled crying method, but the shout it out method often works better when baby is about six months old.

Controlled crying

Many parents worry that baby will be psychologically damaged if he is left to cry. It is always difficult to leave your young baby to cry and settle himself. Your motherly instinct is to go and pick him up. But experience teaches that if you do this every time, he will fall into bad habits and expect to be picked up every time he cries. When you sleep train your baby, it is far more likely that you will be upset than that he will. He will continue to smile at you when you come into his room the next morning and he will still love you.

To be clear, sleep training by controlled crying never means leaving a hungry, wet baby to cry for hours on end. Sleep training means teaching your baby to sleep, because you are concerned for his well-being – now and when he is older. And the whole family will benefit when baby sleeps well at night.

So, when you feel ready to try controlled crying, this is how to do it.

Put baby down in his cot in the usual way. Make sure that he has a full tummy, he doesn't have any wind, and has a clean nappy. Tuck him in, kiss him good night, and leave the room. When he shouts, don't go straight back in. You may find you can only leave him for a minute, but if you can leave him for a little longer than that, it gives him more of a chance to settle himself. If he hasn't settled after about three to five minutes, go in and pick him up. Lift him out of his cot. If he is rooting and obviously hungry, put him back to the breast or offer him another one to two ounces (25–50 g) of milk. If he is not interested, put him on your shoulder and check for wind. When you have tried both these things give him a cuddle, tell him you love him and he needs to go to sleep, then tuck him back in his cot and leave the room.

When he starts shouting again, leave him for longer than you left him the first time. When you go back in, don't take him out of his cot. Stroke his head and say, "Mummy loves you but you're not coming out. It's night nights time." Do this quite quickly, then leave the room. He will probably shout even more loudly when you leave the room this time, but you should leave him for longer than you did the first time. It is most important that you don't pick him up or feed him. This is the start of the process of teaching him that he is not coming out of his cot and he needs to go to sleep.

Each time you feel you need to go into him, make sure that the gap between visits is longer than the previous one. This is to give him the chance to settle himself to sleep. You may have to persist for an hour or so, with him shouting on and off, before he settles into a deep sleep.

You may be up and down for a couple of hours the first night. Very often baby will settle to sleep and after about thirty to forty-five minutes he will wake up again and start shouting. This is because babies naturally sleep deeply for about this long, then enter a light sleep. If this happens when you begin sleep training you will have to start all over again until he learns to settle himself. If he does wake after thirty to forty-five minutes, don't go into him straight away. Leave him for as long as you can. When you do go in, don't stay with him for long, just reassure him that you are there, then leave the room.

If he wakes up when it's getting close to feed time, leave him for another five to ten minutes, but if he doesn't stop shouting, go ahead and give him his feed.

When you use this method, don't forget that it probably won't work in one night, but may take anything from a week to two weeks. However, you will find that there is improvement after a few nights and this will encourage you to go on. You need to be consistent and persevere, as it is well worth the effort in the end.

Many parents feel very anxious about leaving their baby to shout. It goes right against the grain not to pick up a crying baby. However, if you think about why you are doing it and the results you want to achieve, it will help you to be resolved and see it through. You are doing it for his benefit as well as yours.

"Shout it out" or cold turkey

This method is tougher but works more quickly than controlled crying. You settle baby as you do for controlled crying, but only go back in to him once. Then you leave him to shout until he falls asleep. When he has gone to sleep, you may want to go in and check him, but be careful not to disturb him. You should find that he starts sleeping through nights after just a few. This method works best with a baby who is older, nearer to six months than three months. Older babies sometimes understand that you will be coming in and out (if you are using the controlled crying method) and this can disturb them. Like controlled crying, the shout it out method can be upsetting for parents, but do remember that you are doing it for baby's benefit.

Night feeding

By the time your baby is three months old he should be able to sleep through the night from about 10 p.m. to between 6 and 7 a.m. the next morning. However, many babies get stuck in a routine of waking in the night for a feed when they don't need it. This often happens between 3 and 3:30 a.m. If baby is well, has been putting on weight, and now weighs over 10 to 12 lb (4.5 to 5.5 kg), he shouldn't need a feed in the middle of the night.

There are several ways to deal with this and train him to sleep through. You might like to try the controlled crying method. Don't worry about baby being hungry, as he will soon settle to having more in his daytime feeds. Once baby has dropped his night feed he will be much more settled during the day. Some babies drop their night feed very early on – during their first few weeks – but this is not what normally happens. More often a baby of about six to twelve weeks will wake out of habit in the night for a feed. You know he doesn't really need it if he only takes a couple of ounces, then looks at you and smiles and seems to think he's going to have a party!

Whether you chose the controlled crying method or the shout it out method, you should find that within days baby is sleeping through. As always, do persevere, be consistent and it will work.

If you feel you can't face using either of these methods, you could try gradually decreasing the amount of feed you give each night. Try offering some boiled water instead of milk. Gradually cut that down until baby isn't having anything during the night.This method can take a little while longer to work but may be better for you if you feel you can't bear to hear baby shout.

Twins

As I mentioned in the previous chapter, it is essential that twins develop a good feeding and sleeping routine. They need to be awake, feeding, and sleeping at roughly the same time as each other. This is important to ensure that you have some rest time.

If you are having trouble with one twin sleeping or settling, it's perfectly OK to move him into another bedroom. At this age you can use the controlled crying method to help him to settle and sleep for longer. Once he has settled down again, you can move his cot back into the room with the other twin.

You may find that one twin has longer sleeps in the daytime than the other. If this is the case you may need to get the baby who is wide awake up, so that he doesn't disturb the sleeping one. However, twins often have an amazing ability to sleep through the shouting of their brother or sister in the cot beside them.

Settling to sleep on the breast or by being rocked

Lots of mothers get into the habit of rocking or breastfeeding their baby until he is sound asleep, then putting him asleep into his cot. This seems such an easy way to settle baby when he is little, but it creates bad habits. It is better for everyone if baby learns to settle himself to sleep. However, if you are having this problem, don't despair. You can still sort it out.

If you are used to rocking baby to sleep, give him a big cuddle and hold him in to you and maybe sing in his ear. As he gets sleepier, put him in his cot and tuck him in. Stroke his head, then leave the room. Do this every night. Make sure that each night you put him in his cot a little more wakeful than the night before. You may find you need to use the controlled crying method if he shouts and won't settle.

If you used to feed him to sleep, take him off the breast before he goes to sleep. Cuddle him into you, rock him in your arms a little, then put him in his cot. If he shouts, use the controlled crying method. He will learn to self settle but it may take several days.

Case studies

Libby

I contacted Rachel when Rosa was five months old. For several weeks she had been waking up repeatedly in the night.

From the age of eight weeks to seventeen weeks, Rosa wanted a feed at 11 p.m. and would then go through until about 8 a.m. But at seventeen weeks she suddenly started asking for a couple of extra feeds in the early hours. She didn't seem to take much, and I suspected she wasn't actually hungry. She was sleeping in our room, so we had to really tiptoe around, trying not to wake her.

We got into the habit of sleeping with a download of womb sounds on at high volume on the i-speakers. That helped Rosa to get to sleep and also meant we could get into bed without waking her. Rosa was addicted to her dummy, and used to wake up and cry for it anything from five to fifteen times at night after it had fallen out. The experience was like sleeping next to an alarm clock set to snooze! Soon after she began wanting three extra night feeds as well, I started to feel like a zombie. My sleep was repeatedly broken – I don't think I ever got more than twenty minutes at a go. After five weeks of this I got in touch with Rachel.

Rachel advised me to do several things. First, start Rosa on solid food; second, move Rosa's cot into her own room; third, cut out the womb sounds; and fourth, if the above didn't make a difference, try some controlled crying. The last was something we were wary of doing, so we tried all the other ideas first. Rachel also advised us to stop giving Rosa her dummy when she asked for it in the night.

I implemented all the advice, though I added in a few little extra stages to make it as gentle as possible. I was keen to avoid controlled crying if possible. I started Rosa on solid food (baby rice and pureed fruit) the next day. I decided to wean her off the dummy before moving her to her own room, as I felt it was our fault that she was addicted to it in the first place. We did give it to her, after all. And we'd continued to give it to her whenever she asked for it. I'd found it a convenient way of getting her to nap in the daytime.

It took three nights to wean her off it. Every time she asked for the dummy in the night, I let her suckle instead. This was easy enough, as she was still sleeping in a cot beside me at that point. During the daytime I suckled her to sleep, and if she asked for the dummy when she woke during nap time, I let her suckle instead. I wanted her to forget about the dummy. This meant that for two nights I barely got a wink of sleep. I was already a zombie by that stage, so it didn't seem like much of an extra sacrifice, and on the third night she didn't ask for the dummy – just a couple of feeds.

Once she'd forgotten about the dummy I moved her into her own room, and cut out the womb sounds. Immediately I noticed a vast improvement in her sleep. By then Rosa had been on solids for a few days, and was less hungry. I stopped waking her for a feed at 11 p.m. and let her wake up naturally. At first she woke at 2 a.m. instead, but that crept later day by day:

3 a.m., 4 a.m., 5.30 a.m... Within a week she had started sleeping through the night. It was what she had wanted to do all along. I think I had inadvertently been stopping her, with my well-meant but unhelpful habits.

However, I still found it very difficult to get her off to sleep in the first place without the dummy. So because of that I tried some controlled crying. I was amazed at how easy it was. Rosa never cried for more than nine minutes before she drifted off (and that was the first time I tried it), and it was tired crying, rather than "upset" crying.

Rachel's advice has made a huge difference! Mummy and daddy are well-rested, and having Rosa in her own room means that we have our bedroom back. But mainly it's just unbelievably wonderful to be able to count on getting a decent night's sleep most nights.

Joss

Harry was about four months old when I got in touch with Rachel. I was exhausted and struggling to co-ordinate everything, despite having a good feeding pattern with Harry.

He fed at 6:30 a.m., 10:30 a.m., 2:30 p.m., 6:30 p.m., and 11 p.m. However, after 6:30 p.m. he would be restless but not go to sleep. I kept him up until 9 p.m, by which time he was exhausted and would fall asleep. Having to keep him awake during the evening was affecting my spending time and eating with the rest of the family. It was also stressful, as by then it had already been a long day and I just wanted to rest.

Rachel came to stay for one night. She just watched and helped me the first day. On the second day she suggested I put Harry down at 7 p.m. I'd tried this a few times before and it hadn't worked, so I wasn't very confident. However, Rachel gave me the confidence to try again and Harry only cried for a few minutes before going to sleep. This one simple thing gave me the strength to repeat it the following night. I never looked back. Obviously some nights he'd cry and some he wouldn't, but mainly it was a confidence thing for me. And I realized that babies don't sleep better when they have less sleep; they sleep better with lots of sleep at the right times.

Nicola

At about four and a half months Henry started to struggle with daytime naps and woke up more during the night. He had been feeding at 11 p.m. and 4 a.m. but now he would wake at 9 p.m., 12 a.m., 3 a.m., and 6 a.m. Rachel suggested that I should move completely on to formula, as my milk would probably not be satisfying enough as I was so tired. I should also try Henry on some baby rice.

As soon as I gave Henry some solid food he started to sleep much, much better. He gobbled up his baby porridge and hasn't looked back. Although I did my very last breast feed when he was about six months old, I had been reducing and reducing until I was just doing the 11 p.m. feed. Introducing more formula feeds helped both Henry and me. I had more energy, he slept better, and I felt like I was getting a little bit of my life back.

At five and a half months, after a nasty bug, Henry's sleep was really disturbed again. I broke all the rules and just went to him in the night and cuddled and rocked him. When he was one hundred per cent better I realised he had fallen into a habit of needing to be cuddled or fed to sleep. By this time he was eating three solid meals a day (and taking a lot) and also getting formula feeds, so I was very confident that he wasn't hungry. He was calling for me as he simply wasn't able to get back to sleep without help. I was only getting about three or four hours of interrupted sleep a night and was beginning to worry about the neighbours.

As he was waking so often, Henry was crying a lot during the night. I felt as though nothing I was doing was really helping him. Rachel very calmly and gently talked me through how to start controlled crying, which gave me the confidence that this was the right thing to do. She explained that I shouldn't leave things much longer as it is harder to do with a child who can haul himself up in his cot.

The first evening of controlled crying it took Henry over an hour to settle. However – and crucially – I felt that I was doing something positive to help him. Each time I went in to check on him (after three, then five, then ten minutes) I told him I loved him but it was bedtime. Telling him I loved him made something very difficult a lot easier to do. He eventually settled, waking once more that night.

The next day I put him down for his morning nap and after playing in his cot for ten minutes he fell asleep without any problems. He is now a brilliant sleeper and all the happier for it. He also seems to be much better at demonstrating when he is tired, by rubbing his eyes, pulling his ears, and getting cuddly. He didn't always do this before the sleep training. Now I can take him to see friends and family safe in the knowledge that he will fall asleep in his travel cot. It makes his life and mine much, much easier and more enjoyable.

Sleep solutions:
six to twelve months

During the next few months your baby's routine will change so that he will be having three meals a day. His nap times will be slightly different too. Even if baby has no sleep routine or structure in the day or at night, it is not too late to start training him.

Without a good sleep routine for baby, you and your partner will no doubt be very sleep deprived and desperate to have some good nights. Having a baby who doesn't sleep can have a disastrous effect on a relationship: couples find they spend little or no time together, and dad often ends up sleeping in the spare room. It is common for mum to be very weepy and feel that she is not coping. Making any sort of decision can be very hard work. Apart from the effect it has on parents, the baby suffers too. Chronically tired babies never settle to sleep for long and they are often grumpy and fretful. If you are at this stage, remember that sleep training is kind, not cruel, however hard you find it to listen to your baby cry.

You may find it upsetting even to read a book on sleep training, as it seems to be so hard on baby. He is a little person who needs love and care, but he also needs to know the boundaries. Remember that if you are doing full-on sleep training and baby is crying a lot, it is important to make sure that he has lots of cuddles in his wakeful times.

Your baby may have been a good sleeper until about six months of age, then started being unsettled at night. This may be because of teething or illness. It is hard when you have had a good sleeper to know what to do. It is so easy to pick baby straight up and comfort him, when in fact if you leave him he may well settle himself. Whether your baby has been a good or bad sleeper, the important thing is not to rush in and pick him up as soon as he starts to cry.

How much sleep should my baby have in 24 hours?

Your baby should be sleeping for about twelve hours a night and having about two to three hours' sleep in the day. This adds up to about fourteen to fifteen hours in each twenty-four. Please don't give up or feel a failure if he is not achieving this. This chapter is here to help you. Many babies of this age are still having a feed last thing at night and waking in the night for a feed. At six months baby may well be having two good daytime naps, but by the time he is twelve months old it is likely that one of these naps will be shorter than the other. Normally a twelve-month-old will have a short morning nap and a longer nap after an early lunch. However, babies are all different, so don't worry if yours naps at slightly different times. The important thing is that he naps in the day.

Where should my baby sleep?

Ideally your baby should be sleeping in his own room by now. Many parents move baby into his own room before he is six months old. It is more or less impossible to sleep train your baby if he shares your bedroom, so he does need to be in his own room.

If you are worried about moving baby out of your room, remember that it is easier to move him now than it will be when he is older. Some parents just go for it, others wait until a weekend when they are not at work and feel more able to deal with the tears from baby – if there are any. Most babies of this age are perfectly happy to sleep in their own room.

Baby also needs to sleep in his own cot. He will have grown out of the Moses basket or crib by now unless he was premature and very little at birth. He will no longer be swaddled and will probably be sleeping in a Grobag, tucked in with one blanket if the weather is very cold. He doesn't need to have black-out blinds in his room; thick curtains are fine. If baby is only used to black-out blinds it can cause difficulties if you go away and he finds he can't settle unless there is complete darkness. And by the time he is a year old it is good for him to be able to see well enough to sit up in his cot and play when he wakes early in the morning.

Baby should not sleep in your bed. If he sleeps with you all the time he is very likely to develop an attachment problem and find it distressing to be on his own.

It is fine for baby to share a bedroom with a sibling from about the age of six months. He will probably love this, as he will be able to play with his big brother or sister, and it will teach both of them to share. However, when you put a baby of six months or over in a room with an older sibling, especially if the older child is a toddler, you need to make sure that the older child doesn't climb into the cot and squash the baby. Usually, if the toddler is in a Grobag or a sleeping bag without individual legs, he won't be able to climb out of his cot, but some toddlers are real climbers and will get out of anything. As the toddler gets older he will understand that he must look after baby and not get in the cot with him.

During the day

Baby can sleep in his cot in his room for daytime naps when you are not going out. If you have a pram and a garden that is safe for baby to sleep in, it is lovely for him to sleep outside for daytime naps. He does need to be strapped in. Do make sure that you have a cat/insect net for the pram and that your garden is safe from foxes and squirrels. If you have room, he can sleep in his pram indoors when the weather is not good enough for him to be outside. Some babies will happily take short naps in their playpens.

Babies often sleep well on the move or at baby groups. In fact often baby will sleep better out and about than he will at home if he has always been used to being in the car or pushed out. It can be difficult if, when you are at home, he does not settle well in his cot. We will deal with this problem later on.

Baby may also sleep in a sling attached to you. However, he will be too heavy for this now, and it is not good for his back as he needs to sleep flat.

"How to" guide

Below are three sleep and feeding plans that will enable you to understand ideal sleep routines as your baby's needs change through this six-month period. The sleep times are approximate and may change as baby gets older. They are meant to be a guide for you, not hard and fast rules.

Sleep plan from six to around nine months

6 to 7 a.m. Feed baby when he wakes.

If you are reducing breast feeds and doing some bottle-feeds, it's usually a good idea to breastfeed first thing in the morning.

8 to 9 a.m. If your baby is now having three meals a day, give him breakfast: solid food with a drink of milk.

9 to 9:30 a.m. Back in his cot or pram for a short sleep. This nap will probably be about thirty to forty-five minutes long.

10 to 10:30 a.m. Wake baby by 10:30 if he hasn't woken himself.

Play time or time to go out to a group or for a walk.

Some babies have another feed at this time if they are still on four-hourly feeding.

11:30 to 12:30 a.m. Lunch, if baby is having three meals a day.

Some babies won't want any milk at lunchtime, just a drink of water or juice from a cup.

1 to 1:30 p.m. Back in his cot or pram for an afternoon sleep.

Baby may nap for about one to two hours, depending on how long he slept in the morning.

3 to 3:30 p.m. Wake baby – try not to let him sleep later than 4 p.m.

Some babies will have a breast or bottle-feed at this time.

4:30 to 5 p.m. Teatime for baby. Solid food and a drink of milk; either breast or bottle, or out of a cup.

5:30 to 6 p.m. Bath baby.

Wind-down time.

Quiet feed at about 6:30 p.m.

If you are reducing breast feeds and doing some bottle-feeds, it's a good idea to keep this last one before bed as a breast feed.

7 p.m. Settle baby in his cot.

This time can be slightly flexible, but if you are having real difficulties with settling baby, stick to the same time each night.

10 to 11 p.m. (optional)

Some babies will still be having a feed at this time, especially if you are trying to wean them off a middle of the night feed.

By this stage, a night feed is probably just a habit and you may well want to encourage baby to sleep through the night. Details of how to do this can be found later in this chapter.

Sleep plan for nine to twelve months

7 to 7:30 a.m. Wake and get baby up.

Feed, if baby still wants a morning feed.

If baby is not taking much milk from either breast or bottle, it's fine to go straight to breakfast without a morning feed. Make sure he has milk with his breakfast.

8 to 8:30 a.m. Breakfast: solid food.

Baby can also have a bottle or breast feed, or a good drink of milk out of his cup.

9:30 to 10:30 a.m. Baby will be ready for a long morning sleep, which can be in his pram or cot. He will usually sleep for about two hours.

12 to 1:30 p.m. Lunch: solid food and a drink. This can be milk from a bottle or breast, or a drink or water or juice from a cup.

3 to 4 p.m. Afternoon nap.

This may be in his cot or while you are out and about. It doesn't matter if this is just a short nap, especially if baby had a good morning sleep. Wake him up by 4 p.m. as otherwise it can be difficult to settle him for the night by 7 p.m.

4:30 to 5 p.m. Teatime.

Baby can have solid food and a drink of milk or water. Milk can be from the breast or bottle, or in a cup.

5:30 to 6 p.m. Bath time.

Get baby ready for bed. Quiet time and feed.

7 p.m. Settle baby in his cot for the night.

These sleep times are approximate and may change as baby gets older. They are not meant to be hard and fast rules.

Sleep plan for around twelve months

7 to 7:30 a.m. Wake baby if he hasn't woken by 7:30 a.m.

If your baby sleeps longer, by all means have a lie in at the weekends.

Some babies still have a morning feed, but it can mean they don't eat a good breakfast. If this is the case, cut out this feed.

8 to 8:30 a.m. Breakfast.

If baby has not had a morning feed, give a good drink of milk with breakfast.

9:30 to 10 a.m. Nap time.

This will usually be a short sleep, up to forty-five minutes.

Wake baby by 10:30 a.m. if he hasn't woken himself.

12 to 1 p.m. Lunch. Give a drink of water or juice with lunch.

1 to 1:30 p.m. Afternoon nap.

This will be a longer sleep, up to two hours.

Wake baby by 3:30 p.m. if he hasn't woken himself.

5 to 5:30 p.m. Teatime.

6 to 6:30 p.m. Bath time.

Quiet time to settle for the evening.

Feed, if your baby still wants a bedtime feed.

7 to 7:30 p.m. Tuck baby into his cot and settle him for the night.

You may find that as baby approaches his first birthday, his daytime sleeps will change. He will either have a long morning sleep and a late lunch, or an early lunch and later sleep. So, he may sleep till 1:30 p.m. and then have lunch, or have lunch at 11:30 a.m. and sleep from 1 to 3 p.m. Do be flexible as baby changes and develops. However, it is always important to keep to a regular getting-up time and breakfast routine, and a good tea, bath, and bedtime routine. A good structure will help give your child stability in life and should continue for several years.

Mornings

A good morning routine is important, and its benefits will last for a long time. As you may be going back to work, or baby may be going to nursery – and eventually to school – it is useful to get a routine in place. It helps babies and children to know what to expect each day.

Baby may wake up any time from 7 a.m. You may find this becomes 8 a.m. when he is sleeping really well. If you don't have to get up and go out, enjoy not having to hurry.

If baby wakes for the day at 5 a.m, this is too early. This sometimes happens when the mornings get lighter. Try using the controlled crying method to encourage him to go back to sleep. You may find for the first few mornings it doesn't work and he is very tired in the day. But persevere, as he will learn. After a few days he will sleep on till about 7 a.m. – you may even have to wake him up!

Daytime naps

If you are having difficulty settling baby for his daytime naps, it is a good idea to do the same thing every time you put him down. If you do this whenever you are at home, he will become used to the routine. After his feed or meal and some play time, he should be ready for his nap. Sit with him on your lap, look at a book together or sing some nursery rhymes, cuddling him into you. Tell him that he is going in his cot for a nap, give him a kiss, and put him down, tucking him in if necessary. Make sure he has his cuddly toy or muslin, then leave the room, shutting the door behind you.

If you put him in his pram in the garden, he will need to be strapped in and tucked in with a blanket if necessary. Put the cat net onto the pram and push it outside. Rock the pram for a moment or so if he doesn't settle, or take him for a short walk down the road. Babies often settle while on the move but wake up as soon as the movement stops. If this is what your baby does, leave him to shout for a while to see if he will settle by himself. If you do this on a regular basis, you should find that he will learn to settle and sleep well.

Signs of tiredness

As a baby gets older it is easier to spot the telltale signs of tiredness. Baby will rub his eyes, yawn, and turn his head from side to side. He will be grumpy, start to cry, and his eyes will open and close. He will look pale and may suck his fingers or thumb. If you made a note of what time he got up, you will know when he is likely to be ready for a nap. The period of time he stays awake will lengthen as he gets older. By the time he is nine to twelve months old, he will probably be awake for about three hours at a time.

It is important to put your baby down in his cot or pram when he is showing these signs. A baby who doesn't sleep well may show these signs on and off all day, until you get him into a good sleep pattern.

Bedtime

One of the most important parts of sleep training is baby's bedtime routine. Many babies who do not sleep well have never had a proper bedtime routine, so they are not sure where they are and what comes next. Always make sure you have plenty of time for bath time, winding-down time, feed time and bedtime. If you rush things, or if baby is not used to having a structure, it will be harder for him to settle. This is easier said than done if you have older children. But it really does help if you can start bedtime in plenty of time. Maybe ask a friend or relation to come and help if you are on your own with several children. Teatime to bedtime can be a very fractious time, as everyone is tired – including mum.

Settling baby for the night

It is not essential for baby to have a bath every night, but it is a good idea as it sets a routine up for him. A bath will often calm a grumpy and tired baby. It is also a good time to play, chat, and sing together. Once baby is a couple of months old, you can put him in the bath with an older child. If you are worried about the older child splashing too much or getting out of control, only do this on nights when you have an extra adult around to help.

After his bath, dress baby in his nightwear and cuddle him into you as you give him his bottle or breast feed. Many babies will drop off to sleep over this feed, especially if they are not sleeping well. Try to wake him up before you put him in his cot. Give him a cuddle on your shoulder, rubbing his back, singing or chatting quietly to him. Then lay him down on his back in his cot, stroke his head, say good night, and leave the room.

After he has had his feed it is important that baby is not stimulated in any way. He doesn't need games, loud noise, or bright light, and he shouldn't be bounced up and down. He needs cuddles, and peace and quiet in his room with the lights out and the door shut. If you have a rocking nursing chair, sit in it and cuddle him to soothe him before you tuck him down.

How long should my baby take to settle?

By the time your baby is six months old he should be settling by himself quite happily. If he is a good sleeper you may find he chats away to himself in his cot for a little while before he sleeps. As he gets older you may find that he will sing himself to sleep, which is very sweet to listen to. He should be settled within twenty minutes. If he shouts when you put him down, he should be quietening down after twenty minutes. If he doesn't, go into him and reassure him, then leave the room. If you are doing sleep training, proceed with whichever method you are using.

Sleep aids

Many people use a dummy when their baby is newborn but find it difficult to wean him off it. By the time he is six months old he will be fairly attached to his dummy if he has had one from early on. Some parents decide to leave weaning baby off his dummy until he is older, whereas others feel it is a nuisance and prefer to take it away. Whenever you decide to take action, it is likely that baby will make a fuss. He may shout a lot, but you will feel worse than he does. You can start weaning him off the dummy by letting him have it when he settles for a daytime nap and when you put him in his cot in the evening. Don't use it again if he wakes in the night. Gradually wean him off it completely by not letting him have it for daytime naps, then at night too. It all sounds very easy, but some families struggle with this. Another idea is to take it away completely and not use it again. Some parents feel this is too hard, but it does depend rather on how attached baby is to the dummy.

If you are going to let him keep it, as baby gets older the dummy can be attached to his nightclothes with a special dummy clip so that he can retrieve it himself. This saves you having to get up and down in the night to put it back in for him.

Mobiles, blankets, musical toys, and cuddly toys are all good sleep aids and you will probably find your little one will become attached to one or more of these. If you are trying to wean him off his dummy, give him a blanket or cuddly toy to replace it. Make sure you have a spare in case it is lost or for when it needs washing.

Never leave a bottle of milk or juice in baby's cot. He might choke on the bottle and juice is bad for his teeth.

How not to settle your baby

• Don't spend a long time rocking your baby to sleep.

• Don't push him round and round in his pram.

• Don't drive him around in your car.

• Don't breastfeed him until he falls asleep.

• Don't let him sleep too late in the afternoon.

• Don't let him go to bed hungry.

• Don't rush in to him to the moment he shouts.

• Don't overstimulate him before bedtime.

Troubleshooting guide

Some babies are better sleepers than others and some take longer to learn how to settle themselves. Each baby is different – brothers' and sisters' sleep needs can be very different. However, all healthy babies and children need sleep, so don't give up. If you have a special needs child you may find that he doesn't sleep very well, and you may need specialist advice.

Coping with a crying baby

It is especially difficult to cope with a crying baby when you are tired and baby is unsettled. If baby is crying for long periods because you are sleep training, remember that you are doing this for his benefit as well as the benefit of the whole family. However, if it is really getting to you, do ask for help and make sure you get some time out. Share the load with your partner, or ask a parent or friend to sit with the baby or take him for a walk so that you can have some time to think and clear your head. There is nothing like having a couple of hours away from the responsibilities of motherhood to help you feel in control again. If you have no one who can help, take baby out in the pram and go out for coffee or meet friends.

What to do when my baby won't settle

Many babies will not settle when they are put down to sleep in the evening. One reason for this might be that baby has never learned to settle because he is used to being picked up when he cries. Or he may always have been cuddled to sleep or allowed to fall asleep on the breast or with the bottle. Some babies learn to sleep lying on a parent's chest or being tucked up in bed with a parent. Others rely on being pushed round in their pram until they fall asleep.

If this is the case with your baby, it is not too late to sleep train him using either the controlled crying method or the "shout it out" method. These are both fully described in the chapter on babies aged three to six months. The techniques are the same for babies aged six to twelve months. The only difference is that an older baby may stand up in his cot and he may be sick. When you go back into him, lay him down, stroke his head, tell him you love him, but say it's bedtime and he needs to go to sleep. If he has been sick, pick him up, change his clothes and bedding without too much fuss, and settle him down again. Then leave the room.

If he has always been good at settling but has just started being unsettled, there may be other reasons for this. It is important to make sure that baby is not hungry. He should be on solid food by now, but if he isn't, this could be why he is unsettled. If you have been breastfeeding, perhaps you no longer have enough milk. It may not work to introduce a bottle to a baby of this age, so give him extra milk in a cup.

Teething or illness may often lead to a baby having problems settling down to sleep. If teething is the problem, use teething gel or granules and give him Calpol or Nurofen when you settle him in the evening. You may find you need to get up to him for a few nights, but as soon as he has settled down again, go back to your sleep training programme if you need to.

If he is ill, give him lots of cuddles and offer him extra milk or a drink in the night. Not sleeping because of illness should be a short-term problem. As soon as baby is well again, go back to your sleep training programme if he won't settle.

Baby may be waking in the night because he is cold. Make sure the Grobag he is sleeping in is the right tog for the time of year. If the temperature drops very low at night, he may need a heater in his room.

Babies of this age don't usually suffer from colic as they are on solid food and their digestive systems are more developed. If baby had reflux when he was younger, this too should have cleared up by now. If he has food allergies you will no doubt have got them under control, so some of the reasons why he may not have slept well as a new baby should no longer be an issue.

However, baby may not be settling because he is overtired. Babies, like adults, find it very difficult to switch off if they are overtired. Baby may drop off to sleep but his eyelids will keep moving and he will wake very easily. It can take very tired babies a long time to enter a deep sleep. The solution is to try and get baby into his cot before he gets exhausted. Normally once he has gone into a deep sleep in his cot he will stay asleep. Sometimes, though, he will wake up after only thirty to forty minutes. If this happens, start your sleep training routine.

Your baby may start going to nursery during these months. This might unsettle his sleep pattern, especially if you have been his main carer. Sometimes baby will have a late afternoon sleep at nursery and this is why he finds it hard to settle in the evening. If this is happening, do talk to his nursery carer so that they know what is going on.

As your baby reaches a year old he will be very aware of his surroundings. A house move could well disturb his sleep pattern for a while. If this has happened, give him lots of cuddles and reassure him. Spend a little more time with him at bedtime to help him to settle.

Time zones

If you have to travel to a different time zone, let baby feed and sleep when he wants to during the journey. When you get to your destination, adjust his routine to the new time zone as soon as you can. You may find that he wants more sleep in the day and doesn't settle or sleep as well at night for a few nights. But if you let him find his level with sleeping and feeding, he will probably adjust in a couple of days. Babies are very flexible and cope better with large differences in time zones than adults do.

Night feeds

By the time baby is six months old he shouldn't need a night feed unless he is underweight or unwell. If he is unwell, he may need a drink of milk in the night, or you could give him a drink of water.

There are various ways of weaning him off his night feeds. Continue to give him the last feed at about 10 to 11 p.m., then nothing more until 6 or 7 a.m. Use the controlled crying method when he wakes and wants a feed, as this is a habit that needs to be broken.

Another way to cut out night feeds and help baby to sleep through is to reduce the amount that he has in his bottle or the amount of time he has on the breast when he wakes in the night. This method usually takes longer to work than controlled crying, but you may find it less stressful. It is your choice!

Whatever method you use you will find that baby will be a happier and more contented child in the day once he starts sleeping through the night.

Case studies

Philippa

At around three months my little girl was starting to have good long night-time sleeps. But at four months she went back to waking every three hours for a feed. At four and a half months I called Rachel for help. Rachel suggested introducing solids. This worked a treat and my little girl went back to sleeping through the night. However this only lasted a few days. I stuck it out but by the time she was six months I was exhausted. So I called Rachel again.

Rachel explained that waking around 3 to 4 a.m. was more to do with habit than hunger. She suggested I tried the controlled crying method in order to help my little girl settle herself back to sleep. Whenever our little girl cried I felt it to the bone, so the thought of using the controlled crying method on her was heart wrenching. But Rachel gave me the strength and confidence to try it, by reassuring me that it was in my little girl's best interest.

I can't say it wasn't hard. On the worst night I'm not sure who cried the most. I carried on because the thought of caving in and starting again from scratch terrified me. It also helped that when the morning arrived my daughter never showed any signs of distress. My fears of her waking in the morning and looking hurt and abandoned were groundless. It took three nights, but on the fourth night my little girl slept right through from 7 p.m. till 6 a.m. She didn't even wake for her 10 p.m. feed!

There was one night a few weeks later when I had to go through it again. However, after that she went right back to sleeping through. Now that she is twelve months old there are times when her sleep is disturbed and she needs a wee bit of comfort. This is usually when she is unwell, and once she is better she always goes back to sleeping through.

Once my daughter started to sleep through the night it was as though a magic wand had been waved. She began to eat better, having fewer but larger meals. And she began to settle into a routine, which was bliss for all of us.

Nanette

I have two children: Adam is three and Alyssa was eight months old when I called Rachel.

Alyssa was waking up every two or three hours every single night. I put her to bed at 6 p.m. but from 10 p.m. onwards she would wake up at least three or four times and and cry loudly until she was picked up and breastfed. My son's room was opposite hers, and he would wake up too. He was too young to understand what was happening, so I would have to settle him once I'd been in to Alyssa.

I started to sleep in a spare bad in Alyssa's room when she was six months old so that I could get to her quickly before she woke up my son and my husband. We had tried getting him to go into Alyssa in the night, but she would scream louder and louder until I went in and fed her. We were all desperate for sleep. Alyssa had a dummy and she would cry when she couldn't find it. When I went to put it back in her mouth, she cried louder and louder, so I would put her to the breast to get her back to sleep. Sometimes this would only take a few minutes, sometimes it would take up to an hour. She would cry so much when I put her down that I would stand there rocking her for ages.

I realized that her waking had become a habit as she woke at almost the exact same times every night. But I just didn't have the energy to deal with it as I needed to get back to sleep as quickly as I could. I would go to bed at 8:30 p.m., barely seeing my husband, let alone friends or family. It was affecting family life as I was so very tired. I argued with my husband all the time and I think I became quite depressed. I lost all my enthusiasm, all my pleasure in playing with the baby and my son, and I found life totally frustrating. I became quite angry. I just existed to get through the day.

Rachel's advice was that Alyssa's dummy falling out was a big factor in her waking up. She also said that Alyssa did not need feeding in the night. We could get rid of the dummy, stop night feeding, and try the controlled crying method all at once, but Rachel warned that that would probably be very upsetting for all of us. So we decided to stop night feeding and try controlled crying first and deal with the dummy at a later date.

Rachel suggested that my husband should go in to Alyssa while we were doing the controlled crying, as she would want to feed when she saw me. If she was thirsty (which I was worried that she might be) we should offer her water.

However, I decided that I couldn't do it at that stage. Alyssa was only eight months old and she was hardly drinking in the day, no matter how much I offered her breast milk or water. I just didn't feel strong enough to hear her cry and cry. I was too tired to face it. I knew that, much as my husband would try – and had already tried many times – to settle her, she would just cry more and more. I felt it was easier on us all if I went in and fed her as quickly as possible. Then we could all go back to sleep, even if only for a few hours, until she woke again.

Eventually, when Alyssa was eleven months old, I decided to do what Rachel had suggested. My mum had come to stay for four days. I was constantly arguing with my husband, and

I was depressed and resentful. I just wanted everyone to go away and let me sleep. I kept dreaming about booking myself into a hotel for a day or two to get away.

After another awful row I said to my mum, "I can't do this anymore. That's it, no more night feeding. I've had enough." I wasn't even enjoying breastfeeding anymore but it broke my heart to hear Alyssa cry.

However, I was finally determined to start controlled crying. The first few nights were hard, but after that Alyssa settled herself back to sleep very quickly when she woke in the night. I didn't even go into her room to look at her after the second night. After six nights she was sleeping from 6:30 p.m. until just after 6 a.m. It was so much easier than I ever thought it would be and I only wished I had done it before.

I am able to cope much better with my two children, and I feel much happier now that I am getting more sleep. However, I do feel as though I have changed as a result of the prolonged sleepless nights. My patience level is definitely much lower than it used to be.

With hindsight I realize that what was really waking Alyssa up was me going in to her so quickly the minute she stirred. My advice to anyone now would be to wait before you go in when your baby starts crying. I was so worried about the whole house waking up that I rushed in too quickly. That was how the bad habits started.

Sleep solutions: twelve to twenty-four months

It is not uncommon for little ones aged between one and two to still wake regularly several times a night. If this is what is happening to you, don't despair. There is always time to put things right.

If your toddler is still not sleeping, the stress on your relationships will be huge and you will be exhausted. Many women become depressed as a result of sleep deprivation, which is a form of torture. As your baby becomes a toddler and is able to stand up in his cot and vomit, it all becomes even more distressing. It is really important to get the sleeping issues sorted out, for everyone's sake.

Sleeplessness also has an effect on your toddler's well-being, his behaviour, and his physical and mental growth and development. His little body needs sleep and rest so that his immune system can develop and strengthen. Toddlers who don't sleep well can look as though they are living on the edge all the time. It doesn't take much to upset them and they may have a tantrum or dissolve into tears. They find it difficult to settle and difficult to stay asleep as their bodies find it hard to relax. Toddlers who don't sleep will probably not eat well either.

During his second year your toddler will learn to walk: in fact he may already be walking by his first birthday. Once he starts moving around by himself and exploring, he will become tired more quickly than he did before. He may be climbing up the stairs and running around and will start to be able to walk alongside the buggy when you take him out. Fresh air and exercise do help babies and toddlers to sleep, so take your toddler out for walks when you can. If he is grumpy and unsettled, taking him out for a walk will cheer him up.

How much sleep does my toddler need?

Your toddler should be having two sleeps in the day at the start of his second year. During the year, between the ages of one and two, he may well drop one short nap and have one long sleep instead. If he naps for forty-five minutes to an hour in the morning, he should sleep for two hours after lunch. It's a good idea to wake him after an hour in the morning, and try not to let him sleep past about 3:30 p.m. as this might jeopardize his night-time sleeping.

A plan for nap times

If baby wakes between 6 and 7 a.m., he will need to go for his nap between 9:30 and 10:30 a.m.

If he wakes between 7 and 8 a.m., he will need to go for his nap between 10 and 11 a.m.

If baby wakes up from his morning nap at 10 a.m., he will probably need to nap again from about 12:30 until 2:30 to 3 p.m.

If he wakes at 10:30 a.m., he will probably need to nap again from 1 p.m. until about 3 p.m.

If he wakes at 11 a.m., he will probably need to nap again from 2 p.m. until about 3:30 to 4 p.m.

These times are a rough guide and may vary as your toddler gets older.

Night-time

Your toddler should be sleeping for about twelve hours a night, going in his cot at around 7 p.m. and not getting up until about 7 a.m. Some parents reading this may think it'll take a miracle for that to happen! But don't despair. You can teach your child to sleep, but you need to be consistent and persevere and have confidence. Many toddlers go through a stage of waking early, especially when mornings get lighter and summer time comes in the UK. However, five o'clock is to too early to start the day and it is possible to teach your little one that it is not time to get up yet.

Where should my toddler sleep?

If your toddler sleeps in the same room as you, it will be almost impossible to sleep train him. He should be in his own room if possible. So, if you haven't moved your toddler into his own room and you have a bedroom available for him, now is the time to do it. If you don't have another bedroom to put him in you could consider moving into the living room and sleeping on a mattress yourself for a few nights while you train your toddler to sleep. This really does work and is worth it in the long run.

Sharing a bedroom with an older sibling is perfectly OK and often works well once the toddler sleeps through the night.

In the day

During the first year of your baby's life he will have been happy to sleep on the move – in the car, or in his pram or buggy. During this next year it is a good idea to train your toddler to have at least one of his daytime naps in his cot, as he will usually sleep more deeply and for longer if he is not on the move. If your toddler is so used to sleeping on the move that he won't sleep in his cot, see the advice on how to deal with this later in this chapter. Of course, if you have other children and are committed to doing school runs etc, it may be impossible for your toddler to sleep in his cot during the day.

If you have a good-sized pram he can still have his naps in this in the garden during the day before he gets too big. Make sure you strap him in or he will climb out over the side.

What sort of cot should my toddler have?

Your toddler should have his own cot and not sleep in your bed with you. Children who share a parent's bed may become so attached to a parent that they develop behavioural issues and suffer real separation anxiety. This is very unfair on the child and can be very distressing for all of you.

A toddler will sleep better in his own cot – and you will sleep better as well. It is important that his cot is solid and comfortable, as he will be sleeping in it for at least the next year or so. Cot beds with removable sides are very good, as you can take the sides off when your toddler is ready and the cot becomes a bed.

Sleeping aids

Thumb-sucking is a habit that usually begins in the first few months of life. Your toddler is unlikely to develop it now if he hasn't already. It is impossible to stop a baby sucking his thumb when he is in his cot, as he will automatically put his thumb into his mouth when he enters a phase of light sleep. If your toddler does suck his thumb it's probably best to go with it, as it comforts him and may help him settle. As he gets older you can train him not to do it when he is up and about – he is most likely to thumb-suck when he is bored, tired, or watching television. Many children grow out of the habit by themselves.

Dummies

Many parents who have given their baby a dummy want to take it away during this year as they find he has become dependent on it. When you want to take it away, let him have it when you put him in his cot, but take it away as soon as he is asleep. Don't give it back to him if he wakes up. Or you could try using it when he settles in the evening, but not letting him have it for daytime naps. Try to avoid your toddler wandering around with his dummy in and out of his mouth all day – it is bad for his teeth and can hamper speech development.

Mobiles

By the time your toddler is a year old he will be able to stand up in his cot and will probably pull a mobile down, so the days of mobiles are more than likely over. You could hang one from the ceiling if you want him to have one, but they are more suitable for younger babies.

Musical toys

Musical toys are still a useful aid to settling and you can put one on the side in his bedroom or have one attached to his cot.

Blankets and cuddly toys

Your toddler may well already have a blanket or cuddly toy he likes to have with him in his cot. This is particularly useful if you are having difficulty settling him, or if you are in the process of taking his dummy away. Make sure you have a spare one that you can use when the original needs a wash or gets lost. Lots of toddlers become attached to a muslin cloth, which is great as you can have lots of spares. If your child hasn't been used to having a special cuddly to go to sleep with, you may want to introduce one. Tuck it into his neck when you settle him to sleep. If he naps in his buggy, give it to him to hold then as well.

Bottles

Never leave a toddler with a bottle of milk or juice in his cot.

"How to" guide

It is important that your toddler's bedroom is darkened for his sleep times, particularly when you settle him down for the night.

This doesn't mean you need special blackout curtains or blinds. Being in a darkened room helps the release of the hormone melatonin, which, when released, makes us sleepy. A toddler who is calm, relaxed, well fed, and in a quiet, dark room will be more likely to settle down to sleep.

During the day

Settling your toddler down at the right time is important, as if he gets overtired he will be much more difficult to settle. If he has been up and awake for two to three hours he is probably ready for a nap. As he gets older, he will be happy to stay awake for longer and will gradually shift from two daytime naps to one.

When you settle him, make sure his nappy is clean and he is not hungry. You may want to take his day clothes off and pop him in his Grobag. If he is going in his cot, take him to his room, sit him on your lap, and have a cuddle and maybe a little story. Tell him he is going night nights and lay him down in his cot. Talk to him in his cot, telling him that you love him and chatting about what you are going to do together when he has had his sleep. Close the curtains and leave the room.

At night

It is so important to have a good bedtime routine, whatever the age of your toddler. Allow plenty of time. If he is hurried when he is tired he can lose the plot and go into meltdown very quickly. If you are struggling to get your toddler to bed, try starting earlier.

Have a play time downstairs after tea, then get your little one to help you clear up the toys. Take him to his bedroom or the bathroom and let him run around while you get the bath ready and get his nightclothes out. It is good for your toddler to have a bath every night if you can manage this. If he is grumpy, putting him in the bath will almost certainly change his mood and he will be happy to sit there and play.

Take his clothes off and put him in the bath, giving him some toys to play with. Wash him first, while he is happiest, and before he is ready to come out. Play with him, or let him play on his own for a little while. Never leave him unattended, and don't let him get cold.

Take him out, wrap him in his towel and cuddle him, maybe singing nursery rhymes to him. Dress him in his nightclothes. Read a story and give him a bottle or breast feed if you are still doing this. Tell him that you love him and he is going to go into his cot to have a lovely sleep so that he'll be ready for the fun things you are going to do together tomorrow. Close the curtains, put him in his cot, and kiss him good night. Turn out the light and leave the room, shutting the door.

As your toddler gets a bit older you may find he goes through a stage of being frightened of the dark. If this happens you may need to put a little night light in his room or leave the door open until he has gone to sleep.

Dos and don'ts for settling toddlers

• Do ensure that your toddler has had enough to eat.

• Do have a good regular bedtime routine.

• Do ensure he is comfortable in his cot and that it has a good mattress.

• Do put your toddler in his cot before he goes to sleep.

• Do ensure the room temperature is right.

• Do ensure you allow him enough time to wind down before he goes into his cot.

• Do give him cuddles and read a story with him on your lap.

• Do keep loud noises down as much as possible.

• Do try to take him for a walk in the day.

• Don't overstimulate your toddler before bedtime.

• Don't put him in his cot with a hungry tummy.

• Don't let him get overtired.

• Don't put him in a room with no blinds or curtains and expect him to sleep.

• Don't give sugary snacks before bedtime as they will stimulate him rather than quieten him.

• Don't feed your toddler to sleep, either on the breast or with a bottle.

• Don't rush in the moment he cries after you have put him down.

• Don't let your child have a late afternoon nap.

• Don't push your toddler around in his pram or take him out in the car to settle him.

• Don't leave a bottle in his cot for him to settle with.

How do I know when my toddler is tired?

It is usually easier to tell if a toddler is tired than if a young baby is. If your toddler is ready for a sleep or nap he may rub his eyes, yawn, turn his head from side to side, look pale, and be rather grumpy. He may also suck his fists or fingers.

How long will my toddler take to settle?

Your toddler should settle himself to sleep within about fifteen to twenty minutes of being put in his cot. However, if your toddler has not been sleeping well and is not in a good sleep pattern, he could well take longer. If you are sleep training him, he could take much longer – this is explained later in the chapter.

Night feeds

Your toddler does not need a night feed now, but may be waking in the night out of habit to have a feed. You can gradually reduce the amount of feed over about a week, then cut it out completely, or just drop the feed straight away. Don't offer your toddler another drink instead of milk. He doesn't need anything in the night unless he is ill, in which case he may need a drink of water. Use the controlled crying method of sleep training if you need to. Once you have dropped the night feed then don't give in and give him one again.

Early waking

Many toddlers wake early in the morning and expect to get up at 5 a.m. This is much too early to start the day, as it means that everyone is exhausted by ten o'clock. What time you get your toddler up will depend on what you need to do during the day. If you are at home with him and he isn't in nursery early, he doesn't need to get up until 7 to 7:30 a.m.

If he wakes before you want to get him up, don't go into him straight away. He may be happy to sing to himself for a while. Once he starts to shout, and has been doing this for a few minutes, go in to him and lay him back down. Tell him it is night nights time and not time to get up yet. Leave the room and follow either the controlled crying or "shout it out" method (see below). If you do this each morning for several days you should find he will settle back to sleep and then you may even have to wake him up!

If he wakes after six, try putting some toys in his cot so that he can sit and play with them.

Sleep plans for toddlers

These times are a *guide*, not a set of rules, so do be flexible. However, it is a good idea to get your child up at the same time each morning. This builds helpful routine and stability into his days. Some parents prefer to take their toddler straight down to breakfast, as they are often messy once they start feeding themselves. You can wash and dress him after he has eaten.

Bedtime on some nights may be later than others, especially if you have been out. If so, try to be home earlier the next night and don't let your toddler have too many late nights in the week.

Sleep plan: twelve to eighteen months

7 to 7:30 a.m. Get your toddler up and start the day.

7:30 to 8 a.m. Give him breakfast and a good drink of milk, either in a bottle or mug.

9:30 to 10 a.m. Put your toddler down in his cot for a short nap.

10 to 10:30 a.m. Get your toddler up for play time or to go out to a toddler group, etc.

12 to 12:30 a.m. Lunch: a hot meal with a drink of juice or water from a mug (or sandwiches and a hot meal at 5 p.m.). Play time.

1:30 to 2 p.m. Settle your toddler for a nap.

3 to 3:30 p.m. Get your toddler up, even if you have to wake him, unless he has had a bad night and is very tired. Try not to leave him to sleep past 4 p.m.

5 p.m. Teatime. This can be flexible, depending on what you are doing, but try not to leave it later than 5:30 p.m.

6 to 6:30 p.m. Bath time.

7 p.m. Ready for bed; tucked in and settled for the night.

Sleep plan: eighteen months to two years

7 to 7:30 a.m. Get your toddler up.

7:30 to 8 a.m. Breakfast.

It is a good idea to go out and do things in the morning with your toddler, then he can have his sleep in his cot after lunch.

Either **11:30 a.m.** lunch, followed by a sleep from 12:30 p.m. to 2:30 or 3 p.m.; or lunch between **12 noon and 1 p.m.** (probably when your toddler is nearer to two years old) followed by a sleep from 1:30 to 3:30 p.m.

5 p.m. Teatime.

6 p.m. Bath time.

7 p.m. Your toddler will be ready to be tucked in his cot and settled for the night. If he is tired and has just dropped one of his daytime sleeps, he may need settling down earlier. You may find that he needs two sleeps on some days, but not on others. Gradually, as he gets older, he will be happy with one daytime nap.

Troubleshooting guide

It is exhausting and can make the whole family feel miserable if you have a toddler who won't sleep. Very often a toddler who is a bad sleeper will sleep for about half an hour and then wake up, all ready to go again. If this happens in your family, it's time to try some sleep training.

Many toddlers don't settle or sleep because they have developed bad habits that are fairly well established by the age of twelve months. Please don't despair if this is your story: it is not too late to teach your toddler how to settle himself and sleep well. It may take longer than teaching a baby to sleep, and it can be more distressing the older your toddler gets, as he will make more noise and will be able to move about more. But it can be done, and it is worth the effort. Everyone will benefit when your toddler sleeps better: he will be happier and more settled, and you and the rest of the family will be less stressed and exhausted.

Why won't my toddler settle?

Toddlers are often unsettled while they are **teething**. Use teething granules or gel and give him Calpol or Nurofen to ease his discomfort.

Illness – a fever or a tummy bug – will also unsettle a toddler. As with younger babies, if you are worried about your toddler's health, seek medical advice. Don't start sleep training when your toddler is ill – wait until he is perfectly fit again.

It is important that your toddler's room is the **right temperature**, as he will wake if he is either too cold or too hot.

Hunger is another reason why a toddler may not settle to sleep. If he has not eaten a good tea, offer him a banana or small bowl of porridge or cereal before he goes to bed. Don't forget to clean his teeth afterwards.

If your toddler has a painful **nappy rash** he might be unsettled because of this. Use a good barrier cream and consult your GP if the rash starts to bleed.

Your toddler may not be sleeping because he is **overtired**. If you think this is the case, give him lots of cuddles before you put him down in his cot. Remember to settle him earlier the next day if possible so that the same thing doesn't happen again.

He may be in the habit of being **rocked or cuddled to sleep**. Try settling him without doing this, teaching him to go to sleep on his own. If this is difficult, turn to the section on sleep training.

If your toddler has started going to **nursery**, this may well make him unsettled for a while. If you have been at home with him for a year and then he goes to nursery every day, this is a big change in his life. Do talk to the carers at his nursery if you are having real problems with him at home.

All sorts of events can unsettle a toddler and affect their sleeping habits: a **new baby** coming along, a **house move**, or **tragedy at home**.

Most children don't start **dreaming** and being affected by dreams before the age of about two years. If your toddler does dream and wake up frightened, go to him and comfort him. You may need to take him on your lap and give him a cuddle before putting him back to bed. We will talk about this in the following chapters.

Some children do need more sleep than others, and siblings often differ in their sleep needs. However, if both parents are good sleepers, their children will often be similar. Unfortunately, if you've had one good sleeper, it doesn't mean you'll necessarily get another one, although you may do.

Coping with a crying toddler

Many babies sleep well, then suddenly start waking in the night when they are toddlers. This can be a shock if you are used to having good nights.

On the other hand, you may never have had good nights and are on your knees with exhaustion. If you are sleep training your toddler and he is doing a lot of shouting as a result, do remember that it will pass. He will learn how to sleep and you will be so thrilled when he is sleeping through. Do remember that you will feel worse than he does about it all. He won't love you less because you are teaching him to sleep well. If his crying really gets to you, try to go to another part of the house or into the garden for a little while. Maybe ask a friend or relation to come and be with you if your partner is not there to support you.

How to settle your toddler

Many toddlers have very little sleep during the day. This can be exhausting for you as a mother, as well as for him. If your toddler is at nursery, he should be having a good sleep there.

If he isn't, do ask his carer if she can ensure that he goes down in a cot for at least one good sleep. If he doesn't sleep in the day at home then you need to do some sleep training as set out below. It is a good idea to try to establish some structure in his day. He will continue to need a daytime sleep up to the age of two.

Read to him on your lap in his room before you put him down in his cot. Tell him about the fun things you are going to do together when he wakes up. Settle him in his cot and perhaps leave a CD of gentle music for him to listen to.

If your toddler will only settle to sleep on your lap, it is a good idea to try and break this habit. Sometimes this develops if he has been ill and you have resorted to cuddling him to sleep. If you usually cuddle your toddler to sleep, try giving him a little cuddle then put him gently down in his cot in his favourite sleeping position. Rub his head or back, talk to him softly and sing a little song to him, encouraging him to go to sleep. When he is beginning to settle, leave the room.

Other toddlers may not settle unless they are breast fed to sleep. This is a very common habit. Give him a small feed, then cuddle him and lay him down in his cot. Rub his back, or head or side, and sing to him. When he starts to settle, leave the room. Repeat this every time you put him down for a sleep and he will gradually feed less and less until in the end he will probably settle without you. If he doesn't settle on his own after about a week, use a sleep training method.

Time zones

You may wonder how to deal with your toddler's sleep routine if you are travelling to different time zones. It is not easy travelling by plane with a toddler once he is on the move! Let him sleep on the journey when he wants to, even if it is not his normal nap time. When you arrive, let him sleep and feed or eat as he needs to. Gradually, on the first day, adjust his routine to the local time zone, so that by that evening he is ready to go down to sleep, even if it is later than he would at home. If you are travelling to a significantly different time zone you may well find it takes a couple of days for his body clock to adjust. But you may be surprised how quickly he does adjust.

Sleep training methods

There are three main methods of teaching your toddler to sleep. Controlled crying and shout it out or cold turkey are the methods described in this book. It really is your choice to use the method you feel most comfortable with. Some take longer than others to work.

There has been a lot written recently about leaving babies and toddlers to cry or shout, and the psychological damage that it may do to a child. However, sleep training is not the same as leaving a hungry, cold, wet toddler shouting for hours on end. That is abuse and is very wrong. Sleep training is all about teaching your toddler to sleep, in a controlled and loving way. Your toddler will benefit hugely from sleeping well; he will be a happy and contented little person once he sleeps through the night and has enough sleep in the daytime as well. And the whole family will feel better too.

Once you have decided which method you feel comfortable with, you need to be confident that you can do it, be consistent, and persevere. You will be so thrilled once you have achieved it: it is really the first of the loving boundaries you will need to establish for the well-being of your child. By teaching your toddler to sleep you are showing him more love than if you always let him have his own way, which may mean he becomes continually tired and grumpy.

Don't start sleep training if your toddler is ill, if there is a new baby in the home, you have just moved house, or if there has been a tragedy in the home.

Controlled crying

Follow your toddler's bedtime routine (as described above) and put him in his cot, saying good night. Leave the room and shut the door. If he shouts and doesn't settle, leave him for as long as you can, five minutes if possible. Go in and lay him down if he is standing up, tell him calmly that you love him but it is night nights time and he must go to sleep. Leave the room. It is most important that you don't pick him up, cuddle him, or chat lots to him. You are not rewarding him for shouting.

Leave him for longer the next time, about seven to ten minutes, then go in again and do the same as before.

Leave him longer every time in between your visits to him. This may go on for most of the evening if he has never settled on his own before. Eventually he will go to sleep and you may find that he sleeps right through the night.

If you go in and find that he has been sick, take him out and clean him up, then put him back in his cot. This may happen once or twice. It is important that you change him as quickly and as calmly as you can. You could have a clean sheet and a clean set of clothes ready in his room in case you need them. Don't have lots of dialogue with him, just clean him up and put him back in his cot.

If he wakes up in the night, follow the same procedure and eventually he will go to sleep. You will probably find that the first night is the worst and that you will hate hearing him shouting for so long. Do persevere: remember that you are doing the sleep training for his benefit.

If your toddler has previously been a good sleeper and is going through a wakeful stage you may find that using the controlled crying method will work very quickly. In four or five days he may well be sleeping through the night again.

However, if your toddler has never slept through the night you may well find it will take longer to achieve. Give yourselves ten days to two weeks of following the same routine every night. You may find that after a few days your toddler is sleeping much better, but it may take several weeks for him to settle into a good sleeping pattern. Don't despair: all toddlers are different! You can use controlled crying with a toddler who is teething. But if he is ill, stop the sleep training and start again once he is well.

During the day

If your toddler won't settle to sleep in his cot during the day, take him to his room a little earlier than you would normally, cuddle him on your lap, and read a story. Then put him in his cot. Sometimes having some quiet, soothing music on in his room will help him to settle. Close the curtains to help him sleep. If none of this works, use the controlled crying method.

You will probably find that as he settles more at night, his daytime sleeps will also improve.

You may find it is more difficult to sleep train in the day, as on some days he will sleep in his buggy or in the car.

If he is still shouting after forty-five minutes to an hour and this shows no signs of abating, get him up. It will probably be time for lunch, so calm him down and give him his meal, then try again at his next nap time.

"Shout it out" or cold turkey

This method is similar to controlled crying. Follow your toddler's bedtime routine, put him in his cot, and leave the room. When he shouts, leave him for about five minutes, or for as long as you can bear it, then go in to him. Lay him down, tell him you love him but it is night nights time. Leave the room. When he continues to shout, don't go back in unless you need to check him. He may shout for an hour or longer but will eventually go to sleep.

This method often works more quickly than controlled crying, but you have to be strong to be able to do it. You may find that it works better with a toddler than the controlled crying method. Some mothers find that their toddlers are more upset if they keep going in and out of the bedroom than if they are left to shout it out and settle by themselves.

By the time your child is a toddler he may have chronic sleep deprivation and may take some time to learn how to sleep. Toddlers can shout for up to two hours when you first start sleep training and this will be exhausting for you as a parent.

If this is the case, you too will be suffering from sleep deprivation and may need to find some help and support to guide you through this time. Do talk to your health visitor or come to me via my website as I spend a lot of my time giving advice on sleep to mums. You may need help for your whole family and for your relationship with your partner.

Sleep diary

As your toddler gets older, you may want to use a sleep diary. This helps you to see the improvement you are making. When you are up night after night, it can be very difficult in the morning to remember what happened in the night.

Make a note of the time your toddler wakes in the morning, his nap times during the day, and his bedtime. Note down how long it took him to settle in the evening. Then add what his sleep pattern was like during the night. If you are sleep training him, you will be encouraged as you see his sleeping habits improving as the weeks go by.

Twins

If you have twins, the routine for sleep training is exactly the same as for one child. You may need to put them in separate rooms for a while until they both sleep well. Try to ensure that both twins have their daytime naps at the same time, as this will enable you to have a bit of space during the day. Even if one sleeps and the other is awake in his cot, it's important that they both go down at the same time.

Case studies

Navine
My son Omar was sixteen months old when I first called Rachel. He was waking up very frequently during the night, taking a long time to go back to sleep, and always needed to breastfeed in order to settle. He would wake up about two to three hours after going to bed (sometimes even less), then continue to wake up every one to two hours thereafter. He would quite often wake up as soon as I tried to put him back in his cot. He always ended up in bed with us. He wanted to keep breastfeeding all through the night and still woke up frequently.

My husband and I were always exhausted from sleep deprivation. My husband was finding it challenging to work, so he moved to the guest room. Even there he would still hear the baby crying in the night. I couldn't do much after Omar went to bed, since he would always wake up so soon after. I would spend such a long time trying to get him back to sleep that I would eventually give up and stay next to him. At sixteen months he had never slept through the night since the day he was born. He had probably never slept for more than four consecutive hours on any occasion.

Rachel advised me not to rush over and pick Omar up when he woke up. She told me to let him cry for five minutes before going to him. Then, when I did go in, I shouldn't pick him up. I should lay him back down in bed and briefly comfort him, without too much fuss, then leave the room. If he continued to cry, I should wait another five minutes then repeat the same process, gradually increasing the time I left him. Rachel also advised me not to breastfeed him to sleep.

I implemented the advice on that very day. It was easy. I had been told about controlled crying before and had even attempted it a few times, with no success and lots of tears from both me and my baby. The reason it worked this time was that Rachel helped me to understand the benefits to the child. It also made a difference having realistic expectations and being encouraged to believe that it would work eventually. My feelings about using the technique were transformed and I knew it was the best thing I could do for my child. I felt one hundred per cent OK about doing it and I was able to look forward to him sleeping through the night.

I think that because I felt all right about it, Omar did too. From day one of using the controlled crying technique, he would settle back to sleep after five to ten minutes at the most. I only had to go to him a maximum of twice before he settled. For about a week, he would still wake up maybe three to four times a night, but I would only have to go to him once, or not at all. On day three he slept through the night (from 7 p.m. to 6 a.m.) but after that he continued to wake up once or twice. In the second week, I would hear him wake up, but before the five minutes were up he'd settle himself back to sleep and I didn't need to go to him at all.

However, after two weeks, we went away for the weekend and stayed in a hotel. Omar had a cot in our room so it was impossible to get him back to sleep in the same way. He would scream and scream until I picked him up and brought him into bed with us. He seemed to go straight back to his old ways. Because we were in the hotel I had nowhere to go and was worried about keeping the entire floor awake. I didn't feel too bad, though, because I knew that once we were back at home I could start his sleep training again. Knowing that it had worked once, I wasn't worried.

The first couple of nights back home Omar seemed to resist the training more than when we had first started it. But before a week had passed, he was sleeping through the night, only occasionally waking up and settling himself back to sleep within a few minutes.

We're all a lot more rested, including the baby. I feel that he's been doing better overall now that he is sleeping better and I definitely enjoy the free time I have after he goes to bed.

Nicola

Ethan, my seventeen-month-old toddler, woke at the same time every night and would only settle if I gave him a bottle of milk. I had to change his nappy each time because he was drinking so much.

I was so tired that I was ill all the time. It became dangerous for me to drive safely: I kept seeing things and getting migraines. I was snapping at my five-year-old, Freya, and it wasn't fair on her. Ethan was miserable and tired all the time and he didn't eat well either, because he was full of milk.

Ethan had pyloric stenosis and vomited all the time. He had had an emergency operation when he was seven weeks old. All this meant that he was used to being held a lot. My daughter hadn't slept well since birth either. I just hoped Ethan would grow out of it.

Eventually I decided that enough was enough. Rachel told me to be strong and when I went in to him only lay Ethan back down, stroke his head, and then leave the room. I wasn't to give him a bottle or get him out of his cot. Rachel also suggested that I sat Freya down and explained to her what I was going to do, and why. I was prepared to have a rough couple of weeks, but knew that any short-term pain would bring a long-term gain.

In fact, it only took five days. The first night Ethan shouted from about 9:30 p.m. for just over an hour, then he slept till 6 a.m. The second night he shouted from 11 to 11:30 p.m., then slept till 6 a.m. The third night he shouted from 4 a.m. for a while, then slept till 7:45 a.m. On the fourth night he cried for ten minutes and then slept till 5 a.m. From night five onwards he slept from 7 p.m. until 5:30 a.m. Now if he wakes I go in and give him his muslin and lay him back down – and he goes straight to sleep.

We did have some setbacks, as Ethan got a chest infection two weeks into the process, and I needed to get him out of his cot and nurse him. So I started again from scratch when he was well. Within two days Ethan was back to sleeping through the night.

It has made such a difference to family life. I still have to work on Ethan waking at 5:30 a.m., but because we've both had a good block of sleep by then, I can deal with it much better. Freya and I are friends again, Ethan is sleeping better during the day and has a great appetite. He goes to sleep much more quickly at bedtime. I feel empowered now that I am in control of how Ethan sleeps – and he knows I mean business!

Emma

At eighteen months old Sam, my first child, was not keen on the idea of going to bed and staying there. He wanted to stay up with Mummy and Daddy and bedtime was not a happy time.

He was reluctant to go to bed at a reasonable hour, and when he did go he wanted either Phil or me to sit with him while he played. This meant that we didn't get any time together nor did we get the chance to sit down and have a cup of tea in peace!

It was a long-term problem – Sam was a premature baby and had been woken every four hours from birth.

Following Rachel's advice, we started to give Sam a clear bedtime routine. Every evening started with *In the Night Garden*, then we went upstairs, read three stories, and then Mummy and Daddy left the room. If Sam got out of bed we calmly put him back and explained that it was bedtime.

It took about a week to get established. Sam will always try it on at bedtime and some evenings are better than others. He is quite wilful so we have to keep on top of the situation. He is very often more co-operative for other people.

Having the confidence to stick to the routine has made such a difference – and it also gives us some time to sit down in the evening.

Sleep solutions:
two to three years

We all know that a toddler needs to sleep or everyone suffers from his bad behaviour and general crankiness. As a toddler gets older his behaviour problems become more obvious and difficult to deal with if he is not sleeping well. A toddler who doesn't sleep will often not eat well either, and mealtimes can become a battleground where everyone is stressed.

Sleep is also important for general health and well-being and for the development of young bodies and brains. A toddler who sleeps well will cope better with going to nursery or a child minder, or being at home with Mummy. He will also cope better with a new baby sibling in the home, although sometimes this will disrupt his sleep pattern.

Continual sleep deprivation has a huge effect on parents and siblings. We expect broken nights when we have a newborn baby, but if these are still happening when the baby is a toddler, the effect on the general health and well-being of the whole family can be catastrophic. A mum who has been deprived of sleep since her baby was born may well be living on the edge and will very likely to be suffering from anxiety and feeling she is not coping with life.

Chronic sleep deprivation can drive a wedge between partners who never seem to be able to spend any quality time together. They may also disagree on how their toddler should be sleep trained, and this can have a devastating effect on their relationship.

Often toddlers who don't sleep at home will not sleep if they are away from home either. This means it is difficult for them to stay with other family members and can also be tricky if you go away on holiday. However, your toddler may very well sleep well at nursery because all the other children may go for a sleep at the same time.

So, it is vitally important that your toddler does learn to sleep through the night, for everyone's sake.

How much sleep does my toddler need?

By the time your toddler is two to three years old he should be sleeping for twelve hours at night and may still have a two-hour nap in the day. He should be going to sleep at about 7 p.m. and not getting up until 7 a.m. You may of course vary this, depending on your everyday and work commitments and whether your partner wants to see the little one when he comes home from work. However, it is important that your child has about twelve hours sleep most nights.

By the time your toddler is three you may find that he doesn't sleep in the day but chatters away or plays in his cot or bed. It is good for a child to have a rest in the day even if he doesn't sleep. It gives you a break and it teaches him that there are times when it is good just to be still and quiet and look at books or listen to a CD. If a child grows up with this concept he will find it easier to rest when he is in his teens and as an adult. You may find that he only needs a daytime nap once or twice a week by the time he approaches his third birthday.

If he is at nursery, he may not always go down for a nap. It will depend on nursery policy and what they do there. You can always ask the carers if they will put him down to nap if you feel that he needs to have one.

If your child is at home with you, he will probably have lunch at about 12:30 p.m., then go in his cot for a sleep at about 1 to 1:30 p.m. This can of course be flexible if you are out and about: he may sleep in the car or the buggy for his daytime nap. Try not to let him have a late afternoon nap, as this will spoil his bedtime routine and he may not settle as well in the evening.

Where should my toddler sleep?

Your toddler should be sleeping in his own cot or bed in his own bedroom, or sharing a room with siblings. As he nears his third birthday you will probably feel he is ready to sleep in a bed, although some parents prefer not to move their child until he is nearly four. If he starts climbing out of his cot, you should move him as it will be safer for him to be in a bed.

Parents often put their toddler in a bed when they are expecting another baby. If you have a baby on the way, put your toddler into his new bed a few months before the new sibling arrives. This will give him time to settle. However, if he is not quite ready, leave him in his cot for a couple of months after the new baby is born. If you are worried about the changeover, take your toddler with you to choose some bedding for his new bed. Make it exciting and tell him he is very grown-up to be going in his new big bed. You may want to buy a set of bars that tuck under the mattress and will prevent him from falling out of bed in the night.

The move into his new bed may be great fun for him, but you may find that keeping him in it at bedtime and when he wakes in the morning is a different thing altogether! If you are having difficulties with this, turn to the troubleshooting section.

Sleeping aids

Many children go on sucking their thumbs for several years, especially at night. You can stop a child from sucking his thumb in the day, but not at night because his thumb will go into his mouth automatically. Usually children grow out of the habit, although sometimes it may continue until adulthood. Toddlers usually suck their thumb when they are tired, or when they sit down to watch TV or have a story read to them. If their thumb-sucking is causing orthodontic problems you may need to encourage them to stop during the daytime.

Dummies

At this age dummies are more of a hindrance than a help. They are unhygienic, bad for your child's teeth, and may hinder their speech development. Now is the time to take your toddler's dummy away. Some mums tell their toddler that the dummy is going to the dummy fairy, then pack it up and put it in the bin! If you want to take the dummy away gradually, you can use it to settle your toddler but not let him have it at any other time during the day.

However, if you have a new baby in the home you may feel that now is not the appropriate time to remove your toddler's dummy, especially if he can see that the new baby has one.

Cuddlies

Many children have cuddly toys and blankets to help them settle to sleep and this is a helpful habit. Do make sure you have a couple of replacements, for times when the original needs washing or gets lost. There is nothing worse than losing your toddler's favourite cuddly.

Drinks at night

Never leave a bottle in a cot to settle a toddler, or for him to help himself to in the night or morning. A child of two to three years of age doesn't need a drink in the night unless he is ill, and then he only needs water. If this is a habit you need to break, explain that he can have a drink before he goes to bed, and another one when he gets up in the morning. If you are trying to get him to be dry at night, don't give him a drink after 6 p.m. unless he is ill and running a temperature.

"How to" guide

Your toddler will only need one nap in the day now, and by the time he gets to three years old he may not need a daytime sleep at all. Most toddlers aged between two and three will go in their cot or bed for a nap at about 1 p.m. and rest or sleep for up to two hours.

Settling in the day

While your toddler is still having a daytime nap, it is important to have some sort of structure in his day so that he knows when nap time is. If your toddler has never had a good nap time routine, it will probably be difficult to implement and will take a while to do. You may feel it is not worth the battle at this stage, as he will grow out of daytime naps before long in any case. However, if you do still want your toddler to nap – perhaps if you have a new baby – it is worth getting a routine in place to help him settle.

Make sure your toddler isn't hungry when you put him down to sleep. Give him a snack before nap time, unless he has just had his lunch. Children often feel sleepy after a meal and this is a good time to put him down. Cuddle him and read a story, then tell him he is going to have a lovely rest and go to sleep. Tell him what you are going to do together when he wakes up. Put him in his bed or cot, give him his cuddly toys, kiss him, and leave the room. If your toddler hasn't been used to napping you could put a music CD on for him to listen to; if he is nearly three and not sleeping every day then a music or story CD is a good idea.

Some toddlers are dry in the day at the age of two. However, it is a good idea to put pull-ups or a nappy on him when he has his rest. Otherwise, if he does a wee as he wakes you'll have a wet cot to deal with and he may be upset.

How to settle at night

It usually works well to bath a child before bedtime. This isn't always practical if you have been working, or out, or if you have older children who may need collecting from after-school activities. But if you are able to bath your toddler it will help establish a good bedtime routine for him. Particularly if he hasn't been settling, having the same routine every day will help him learn what to expect.

Let your toddler have a good play time in the bath, then get him out, wrap him in a towel, and sit him on your lap and cuddle him, chatting and maybe singing songs to him.

Put his nightclothes on, take him into his room and sit and read a story to him. Decide how many stories you are going to read and tell him before you start, as toddlers often ask for "just one more!" Explain to him that when you have finished reading he is going to bed as it is night nights time.

Put him in his cot or bed, talking about what you are going to do tomorrow. Tell him that you are going to go to bed yourself too very soon. Kiss him good night, leave the room, and shut the door. You may leave a small night light on if he wants one – it is quite normal for some children to be afraid of the dark.

How to help your toddler sleep

• Do ensure he has had enough to eat.

• Do have a good regular bedtime routine.

• Do ensure he is comfortable in his bed or cot and that it has a good mattress.

• Do put your toddler in his cot or bed before he goes to sleep.

• Do ensure the room temperature is right.

• Do ensure you have enough time for winding down before he goes into his cot.

• Do give him cuddles and read a story with him on your lap.

• Do keep loud noises down as much as possible.

• Make sure he has plenty of fresh air and do try to take him for a walk in the day.

- Ensure he has a good daytime nap if he needs one.

- Try and maintain a calm home environment at bedtime.

Things not do when settling your toddler

- Don't overstimulate your toddler before bedtime.

- Don't put him in his cot with a hungry tummy.

- Don't let him get overtired.

- Don't put him in a room with no blinds or curtains and expect him to sleep.

- Don't give sugary or caffeine-containing snacks before bedtime.

- Don't feed your toddler to sleep either on the breast or with a bottle.

- Don't rush in the moment he cries.

- Don't let your child have a late afternoon nap.

- Don't push your toddler around in his pram or take him out in the car to settle him.

- Don't leave a bottle in his cot.

- Don't let your toddler climb into bed with you during the night.

- If your toddler hasn't eaten a good tea, give him a snack such as a banana or small bowl of porridge before bed. However, make sure he doesn't think that he will get a snack every night if he doesn't eat his tea. Don't forget to clean his teeth afterwards.

Signs of tiredness

Your toddler will show signs of tiredness in a variety of ways.
You will recognize many of them as he will have shown them
since he was a baby. The most common sign is grumpiness
and dissolving into tears very easily. He will probably lose
interest in what he is doing and not be able to concentrate
on playing. He will rub his eyes and yawn and look pale, and
suck his thumb or fingers and hold on tight to his cuddly toy.
He may even go to the sofa or the floor and lie on his tummy
or roll over and over and start to doze off. Some toddlers will
lay their heads on the table and go to sleep at a mealtime.

If your toddler has not slept well at night then he may well
be tired after being up for about two hours. It is sensible then
to put him down for an early nap, even if it is not quite nap
time. If your toddler is ill, then do put him back in his cot or
bed whenever he shows signs of tiredness. Sometimes he will
sleep on and off all day when he is ill: this is fine as the extra
sleep will help him to recover.

A good bedtime routine

A good bedtime routine is vital to help your toddler settle and
sleep well. If you are struggling with this, start bath time and
bedtime earlier so that you have time to make it fun and your
child enjoys the whole thing.

Before you go up to the bathroom, get your toddler to
help you clear up his toys and tidy the room. Then take
him upstairs, get his nightclothes ready, and run his bath.
Have plenty of time for play in the bath. If you have a baby
as well, you can put them both in together or bath baby first
and then put your toddler in while you dress baby. Lots of
mums struggle with this when they have a newborn and it

does take some working out. But your toddler does have to get used to the fact there is now another little person who needs your attention. If your toddler is grumpy, put him in the bath first and then undress and bath baby with your toddler. If this isn't possible because your toddler is splashing and cross, bath your baby in the basin while he is still small enough. Dry and dress your baby and lay him down in his cot or on his mat in the bathroom with you. Then you can finish bathing your toddler. You may need to give your baby part of his feed if he is very fractious while your toddler is in the bath.

If your toddler is happy to play when you go to the bathroom, bath your baby first, then put your toddler in the bath. If baby is then ready to be fed you can feed him in the bathroom while your toddler is playing in the bath. Do be flexible, as what works one night may not necessarily work every night.

Take your toddler out of the bath before he gets cold and cuddle him on your lap in a towel. Put his nightclothes on and read a story aloud with him on your lap. Some toddlers like to sit and be cuddled, others want to rush around the room and not sit quietly. If this is the case, hold him in tight to you and rock him gently. This may help calm him down and then he will be able to settle to listen to a story. If it doesn't work, put him in his cot or bed and read to him while he is standing up. If none of this works, tell him firmly and calmly that you are going to kiss him good night and leave him to go to sleep. Give him a big hug, lay him down, and leave the room.

If your toddler is very tired but will not sit still and have cuddles, try singing nursery rhymes to him. Toddlers love rhymes, particularly if there are actions to go with them.

You may find that your toddler will run away from you as soon as you mention bed, and will want to play games. This can become exhausting, especially if you have a baby to deal with as well. You may also find that your toddler refuses to go in his cot or bed. This may happen suddenly and is a bit of a shock if he has previously been good at bedtime. Look at the troubleshooting section for ideas about dealing with this.

How long will it take for my toddler to settle?

Your toddler should settle himself to sleep within about twenty minutes of you putting him in his cot or bed. However, you may find that on some nights it takes longer. The reason may be that he has had a late afternoon nap. He may have got very excited before bedtime, he may be very overtired, or he may be going down with a bug or virus.

As your toddler gets more mobile, and particularly when he has transferred into a bed, you may find that it takes him longer to settle to sleep. In the summer, when the evenings are light, many toddlers and children don't settle nearly as quickly as they do in the winter.

You may find that your toddler becomes expert in delaying tactics when he finds it difficult to settle. This is quite normal. Have a look at the troubleshooting section for suggestions for dealing with this.

Twins

If your twins are having problems with sleep at night or naps in the daytime, you can use the same methods of sleep training as you would for a single child. If you have one twin who is especially difficult to settle, put him in a different bedroom if possible. As soon as the problem is sorted you can put them back in together. Often twins of this age don't like to be separated, so the threat of separation may be enough to encourage him to settle down.

Troubleshooting guide

If your toddler has been a bad sleeper since he was born it is very likely he will still not settle to sleep well in the evening. On the other hand, it is quite common for a toddler who has been a good sleeper to suddenly start not settling. This can come as a bit of a shock to his parents!

Whatever your situation, if your toddler is currently having difficulty settling, it is a good idea to talk to him about the issue. Explain that he needs to go to sleep and mummy is going to try and teach him how to have good nights, just like she does. This conversation will mean more to him as he gets nearer to three years old. It is still worth talking to your child even if you think he's too young to understand. Of course it is important that it doesn't become a big issue. Try to keep it as something that is positive and fun. You might like to begin a rewards system to help motivate your toddler.

Tantrums at bedtime

Your toddler may have been really happy to have a bath and go to bed, then all of a sudden he starts making a fuss and throwing himself on the floor and shouting at the mere mention of bedtime. Don't worry if this happens: lots of toddlers do it and it will pass. A good solution can be to take him upstairs fifteen minutes earlier than usual, so you have time for him to have a play and he won't feel rushed.

If he continues to make a fuss, one way of dealing with it is to take no notice. Keep going with his bath time routine, undress him, talk to him, and perhaps tell him a story. When you've got him in the bath, blow soap bubbles or play pretend games with his bath toys to try to take his mind off his temper.

The other way of dealing with temper is to talk to him about it. Tell him that his bad behaviour makes you very sad, and promise him reward stickers if he is a good boy.

If he continues to make a fuss about going to bed, try to reason with him and find out what the matter is. Tell him that everyone has to go to bed and he needs to go to sleep so that he can have a lovely day tomorrow.

It is usually a good idea to talk to older toddlers and to explain that their behaviour is not acceptable and you are not going to tolerate it. The best time to talk to them is before they have a wobbly, or afterwards, as they don't really take it in when they are in the middle of a tantrum.

The roving toddler

If your toddler is in a bed but continually gets out and comes downstairs, you need to be firm and set boundaries. He may come down to tell you that he wants a drink or needs to do a wee, or any other excuse. Many toddlers do this when they first go into a bed, and you wish you had kept them in a cot!

When he appears, take him straight back to bed, tuck him in, give him his cuddly toy and tell him he is to stay in bed or you will shut the door. Talk to him and explain that he needs to stay there and go to sleep and then you will do some fun things together in the morning. Many children don't like having the door closed, so this will be a deterrent. If you don't want to close the door, put a stair gate up so that he can't get out of his room. It is important to establish a boundary that he can't keep crossing.

It is perfectly OK to leave him to settle himself in his room. When you shut the door, listen outside and you may hear him playing. If he is happy and singing, as some toddlers do, leave him. He may curl up on the floor by the door and go to sleep. If he does, lift him up, put him back in his bed, and tuck him in.

If he shouts and cries when you shut the door, leave him for five to ten minutes or so. Then go in and tell him that if he is quiet and settles down to sleep you will leave the door open. If he comes out again, warn him that you will shut the door until he is quiet and settles down to sleep. If he continues to shout, don't go back in. Leave him to settle himself. This may take a while, especially if he has been a bad settler.

If he gets very upset, is not settling at all, and you feel you can't leave him, go in. Tell him that you will leave the door open, but only if he is quiet and settles down. You may find that this works if he has been shouting for a while. If it doesn't, then close the door and leave him to settle by himself.

The next night is likely to be better and he will probably settle more quickly.

Try not to worry, as this is a phase that will soon pass and he will learn to settle in his bed by himself.

If you are using a stair gate, make sure he can't watch you through it and see what you are doing. If he can, he may shout and want to come out, so it's important he can't see you. If he tries to climb over the top, you must take the stair gate away, in case he hurts himself, and shut his door instead. He may sit down by the gate and play with his toys, then go to sleep. Pick him up if he does, and tuck him in his bed.

Breaking bad habits

If your toddler will only settle if he is rocked to sleep, sleeps in his parents' bed, or has a bottle or breast feed, it is not too late to break these habits. However, all of them are best tackled sooner rather than later.

If he is still sleeping in your bed, you either need to buy a cot that is large enough to last him for a good few months, or you could put him straight into a bed of his own. He may be really excited by having his own bed and make the transition easily, or it may take him a while to settle into the new arrangement.

He needs to be in his own room as well. You can move him immediately you have a cot or bed for him. Make his room a special place where he has his teddies and cuddly toys, put some pictures on the wall, hang his clothes up in the cupboard, and take him with you to buy his new bedding. You may be surprised how easy the transition is. Once it has happened, don't go backwards by taking your toddler back into your bed again. He needs to forget all about that and be happy in his own surroundings.

If you are settling him with a breast feed or a bottle, remember that he doesn't need either of these things any more. You are not depriving him by taking them away. You can decide either to stop immediately or you could gradually cut down the amount of milk he is having in his bottle, or the length of time you let him suckle. He may well make a real fuss for the first few nights, but he will soon forget and you will be so pleased that you have done it. Offer him a drink of milk from a cup before you clean his teeth. If he doesn't want it, then don't insist, just take the cup away, clean his teeth, and settle him in his cot or bed.

Follow your usual bedtime routine, kiss him good night, and tell him you are going to go downstairs and he is going to go to sleep. Remind him of any reward you may have talked about giving him for settling and sleeping well. Leave the room and shut the door, or keep it slightly open if you are more comfortable with that. However, it is better if the door is closed, as you are putting down a clear boundary for your child.

If you have got into the habit of rocking your child to sleep, this can be a difficult habit to break and you need to do it gently. Rock your child and cuddle him into you for a few minutes, then tell him you are putting him in his cot or bed to sleep. Put him down if he is in a cot, stroke his head, and sing a lullaby to him to calm him. If he is in a bed, tuck him in and kneel on the floor by the bed and stroke his head, encouraging him to go to sleep. You may find you have to do this for several nights until he settles on his own.

If your child doesn't settle, use the controlled crying method. It is important that once you start any sleep training method, you see it through and use it every night. Be consistent.

Only mummy will do

Some toddlers will make a fuss if someone other than his main carer puts him to bed. It is good for him to get used to either parent putting him to bed, if possible. It helps if you both follow the same bedtime routine. This can pay dividends later, for instance if mum has to go away for work or goes into hospital to have another baby. It can be very upsetting if your toddler doesn't want one or other parent to put him to bed, but it is only a phase and it doesn't mean that he loves you any less than he loves the other parent.

The toddler who keeps waking up

If your toddler still wakes every hour or so at night, you will be exhausted. It is not too late to use a sleep training method, but any method you chose may take some time to work. You can find details of the controlled crying and the "shout it out" methods later in this chaper.

If he sleeps in a cot at night, don't take him out unless he has been sick and you need to clean him up. Don't give him a drink at night – he doesn't need one unless he is ill and has a fever.

If your toddler now sleeps in a bed but keeps waking in the night and coming into your room, this is a habit you need to break. You may have taken him into your bed as this seemed the easiest solution at the time. Don't feel guilty about doing this – but don't let it become a habit.

When he wakes up and comes into your room, get up and give him a cuddle if he has woken up distressed and dreaming. Take him back to his room and put him back into his bed. Stroke his head, tell him that everyone is asleep, and that he needs to rest and sleep too. Leave the room and shut his door.

If he is not distressed when he appears by your bedside, keep putting him back in his bed and shutting his door. It will help if you chat about this with him during the day. Calmly explain that you will close his bedroom door if he keeps coming out of his room at night. Children can fall down the stairs easily in the night so you might want to put a stair gate up and leave the landing light on low to prevent any accidents.

If he keeps getting out of bed, coming to the door, and shouting for you, consider using the controlled crying method.

If you don't like shutting his door, use a stair gate at the doorway of his room. Once you have set a boundary he will know that you mean business. If he shouts and shouts and wakes the rest of the family, it is better if you can bring yourself to close his door.

The early bird

Lots of toddlers start waking early as they get bigger, especially when the mornings are light. It is important that you don't get your toddler out of his cot or let him run around before you are ready to start the day.

If your child is still in a cot, put a few soft toys and little books in his cot before you go to bed so that he has something to play with when he wakes up. You could keep these as special toys that he has just in his cot in the mornings and doesn't play with during the rest of the day. Make sure there is enough light coming in so that he can see to play.

If he wakes and shouts, go into him and tell him it is not time to get up and he must stay in his cot. If you do this each morning, after about a week he will not make a fuss when he wakes up. He will have learned that he is not getting up until you are ready. Often toddlers will wake at 5 a.m. then go back to sleep.

If your toddler is in a bed, I would buy a clock where the light comes on or, for example, the rabbit ears come up when it is time for him to get up. Then you can set it to the time when you want him to come out of his bedroom. If he keeps coming into your room too early, get up and take him back every time and shut his bedroom door if necessary. He will soon learn that he has to stay in his room until you are ready for him to start the day.

The night-time snacker

Toddlers don't need to have a drink in the night unless they are ill or teething. If your child is distressed and needs a drink, give him one, but don't make a habit of this. Only give him water, not juice or milk. He doesn't need any food in the night as this will take away his appetite in the day. Don't be tempted to give him snacks just to keep him quiet, as this will be bad for his teeth and also set up bad habits. Keep water and medication upstairs so that they are nearby when needed.

Reasons for not sleeping at night

There are many reasons why a toddler doesn't sleep. If he is really overtired, he may nap for thirty minutes or so, then wake up. This is very common in children who have always had difficulty settling and sleeping. Their little bodies and minds are not used to relaxing thoroughly and switching off.

The most common reason for a toddler not sleeping is that he has never learned to settle and sleep on his own. It can be a lonely place to be if you are the parent of a child who doesn't settle, and you will be worn out yourself with all the disturbed and sleepless nights. I believe that coping with a crying baby, toddler, or child when they won't sleep it is one of the most difficult things to do to. If you have never had a good night since your toddler was born, you will be feeling at the end of your tether and not functioning properly. You will feel as though you are living on the edge and not coping with life. Your marriage or relationship will be under huge strain. It is important to seek help and speak to your GP about this as you need as much support and help that you can get.

If you have a mum or relation or close friend nearby, do ask them to come and help so that you can get a rest, or even go away for a night or so. You may find that when someone else puts your toddler to bed, he sleeps much better.

If you are pregnant again and your toddler isn't sleeping it is particularly hard, so get help if you can. It is important that you get some rest.

If you are back at work you may well feel exhausted, so try to make sure that you get some rest and time on your own over the weekend.

However, even if your toddler has never slept well, it is not too late to teach him, so don't despair.

Check that your toddler isn't sleeping too much during the day. You may need to restructure his daytime naps, or he may be reaching the stage when he doesn't need a sleep every day. It is good to keep up the habit of your toddler going to his room for an hour during the day for some quiet time, even if he doesn't sleep every time.

If your toddler is **ill or teething**, he is likely to suffer from disturbed nights. If he is teething, you may need to get up to him, rub some teething granules on his gums, or give him some Calpol or Nurofen. You may need to get him up and give him a cuddle, but settle him back down again straight away. You don't want him to think that being up in the night is all a bit of fun!

If he is ill, don't try to sleep train him until he is better.

Toddlers will often have disturbed nights if there is a **trauma** or a **big change at home**. A **house move**, a **relationship break-up**, **illness in the family**, or even **stress** brought on through **financial problems**, can all affect your toddler. Often a toddler will start waking in the night when you have **another baby**. He may stir when he hears you up and about feeding, or he may just wake because he is feeling unsettled because there is another little person in the house. Babies, toddlers, and young children will all need lots of cuddles and reassurance in the daytime if you are going through any of these events.

If he has just started at **nursery**, he may be taking a while to be away from you and settle in. If this is the case, he needs lots of cuddles and attention when he comes home. It may also help if you can spend more time with him at bedtime.

He may also wake if he is starting to have **dreams** or **nightmares**. This tends to start happening between the ages of two and three. Sometimes your toddler will wake after a couple of hours, distressed and not really knowing where he is. Always comfort a child who wakes up distressed – this is a phase and he will grow out of it. If he wakes and is scared and upset, go in to him, put him on your lap for a cuddle, and soothe him, stroking his head. He may not be able to tell you what the trouble is, but as soon as he is calm, put him back in his cot or bed, telling him that everything is all right. You don't need to find out about the dream – all he needs is for you to comfort him. An older child may tell you about the dream in the morning.

Younger toddlers aren't usually **afraid of the dark**, but by the time your child is nearly three he may be saying that he wants a light left on in his bedroom. This can be a very real fear, so it's best not to battle it. Either leave his door open with the landing light on, or buy a plug-in night light for his room. His imagination is developing all the time at this age, so remember not to let him watch television or DVDs that aren't suitable for him. He will remember scary images and may think he sees wild animals or horrid faces in the dark. Always reassure a frightened child: give him lots of cuddles and tell him you are not far away, so that he feels safe and secure.

Many children **sleepwalk**. If your toddler has started doing this, make sure that he is safe and can't fall out of a window or down the stairs. Clear his bedroom of toys before he goes to sleep, in case he trips over on them or accidentally damages his favourite. Don't try and wake a sleepwalking child, just give him a cuddle and put him back to bed.

Check the t**emperature in his bedroom**, as your toddler may be waking because he is too cold or uncomfortably hot.

Nappies and sleep

Your toddler may not be dry at night before the age of three, but you don't need to worry about that yet. You may find he wakes with a very wet nappy in the morning. By the time he is about three years old he may be dry some nights but needs to do a wee as soon as he gets up.

Lots of toddlers do a dirty nappy early in the morning and will stand up in their cot and shout because they are uncomfortable. The best thing to do when this happens is get up and change your child's nappy, then settle him back in his cot again. He may make a fuss, but give him a big cuddle, tell him it is not time to get up yet, put some toys and little books in his cot, and leave him to settle down again. You may find you have to go in and out for a while, but after a day or so if he is waking regularly with a dirty nappy, he will learn that he has to go back in his cot after being changed.

Travelling or changing time zones

If you are going in and out of different time zones, this is likely to upset your toddler's sleeping habits. If you are staying in the same time zone for a while, adjust his routine to that time zone as soon as you can. You may find that he needs an extra nap or so in the day and needs to stay up a bit later at night until his body clock settles down. It is a good idea to wake him for breakfast, then he can start the day with you, but you may need to be flexible, depending on how far the time zone is from the one you have left. If you are on holiday and he is grumpy because of different nap times or because he hasn't had enough sleep at night, put him down in his cot or bed for a nap. It is miserable for little children to have to keep going when they are exhausted.

Sleep training methods

Both the controlled crying and the "shout it out" methods of sleep training involve leaving your child to cry. Much has been written about the rights and wrongs of this. If you combine either of these methods with lots of cuddles and love and care during the day, you are not neglecting your child and he will not be psychologically damaged. Usually, the parents find the process of sleep training more upsetting than the child does. Sleep training is not the same as leaving a cold, hungry, wet child to cry for hours: that is abuse and is always wrong.

Controlled crying

When a child is two to three years old, you can chat to him about what sleep training is and why you are going to do it. He will understand lots of what is going on and will know that he needs to settle and go to sleep. You can give him rewards for settling well and sleeping well. The most important thing is to persevere and be consistent.

If your toddler is still in his cot, it is much easier to train him as he can't get out. Obviously as a child gets bigger and older he will make much more noise. Once he is out of his cot and in a bed he can move around and come out of his bedroom.

When you start sleep training, follow his normal bath and bedtime routine. Settle him in his bed or cot, leave the room, and shut the door. If he cries, leave him to shout for as long as you feel you can. This may be only two minutes, or it may be longer. When you go back into his room, lay him back down and tell him it is night nights time and he is to go to sleep. Don't have a long conversation with him. Leave the room, shutting the door behind you.

Leave him as long as you feel you can, but make sure it is longer than the first time. Go in again and put him back to bed or resettle him in his cot. Don't spend very long with him. If he has been sick, clean him up and change him and put him back down. Don't make a fuss of him.

Leave him for even longer the next time. You may find that it is better not to go in often, as that may unsettle him even more. When all is quiet, have a peep at him to see if he has gone to sleep. He is only likely to be sick once or twice; usually children stop after a night or so.

You may find you have to follow this procedure night after night for a couple of weeks. It is quite normal for a child to make good progress for a few nights then have a patch of bad nights again. Do persevere, as he will eventually settle down and start sleeping through the night.

You may find that in two or three nights he is sleeping through and the problem is solved. There is no way of telling how each individual toddler will react.

"Shout it out" or cold turkey

This method works quickly but not every parent feels that they can carry it out. Leave your toddler to shout for as long as you feel you can. This may be two minutes, or it may be five. Then go in to him, lay him down, and stroke his head. Tell him it is night nights time, and leave the room. After this, don't go in to him again. He may shout on and off for an hour or so and then go quiet. At this stage you may want to peep in at him and make sure he has gone to sleep. But be careful not to disturb him, as if he sees you he will start shouting again.

If you persevere with this method you will probably find that he will be settling and sleeping well after just a few nights. But you do have to be strong to carry this out, as there will be a lot of shouting, which you might find distressing.

Whichever method you use, you will be thrilled when your toddler is sleeping. It will make a tremendous difference to family life. Do remember that you are showing love to your toddler by teaching him to sleep. He will be so much happier once he starts sleeping well.

Sleep diary

It is a good idea to keep a sleep diary in which to record the times your toddler sleeps and how long it takes him to settle. This will enable you to see his progress as you sleep train him. When you are in the middle of it all it can be difficult to remember exactly what did happen in the middle of the night.

Common problems

Having a new baby and a toddler who doesn't sleep is one of the most exhausting things that you can go through. Be consistent with sleep training your toddler and don't worry that it will wake your new baby. A newborn won't be woken up by an older toddler crying, however loud it seems to you. Any sleep and rest you can get in the day will help you to keep going through the bad nights.

When you have two or three children and are on your own at bedtime it can sometimes feel as if you are being pulled in all directions. If possible, find someone to come and help you at teatime and bedtime, at least occasionally. It will make a huge difference.

You may like to try starting tea and bed about fifteen minutes earlier than usual, to give everyone more time. Children do pick up when their carer is feeling pressured and stressed, so try to keep everything as calm as possible.

If your toddler has been ill, this can throw his sleep pattern out completely. As soon as he is well again, try gently and lovingly to put in a sleep routine in place again. This may take a bit of perseverance on your part, but it is well worth it and your child will benefit hugely from being back in a good sleep pattern.

The most important thing is to keep chatting to him and explaining that it's important for him to sleep, and that mummy and daddy love him very much. This will help him to feel secure in what you are doing. Very often a child who has been ill has been given lots of extra attention and it can be tricky for him to understand that now he needs to go back to settling himself. If you're having trouble with sleep after a period of illness, then use the sleep training methods outlined above.

Case studies

Piera

Sophia, who was two years and nine months old, had recently started a new nursery. She used to sleep pretty well but she suddenly started waking at 5 a.m. and calling out and screaming. She also began crying when I put her to bed.

When Sophia is not getting enough sleep her moods bring the whole household down and the whole family was tired and grumpy. I also had a new baby, who was now five months old, so I felt that Sophia's problem was probably a short term issue – a combination of a new baby in the house and the new nursery.

I kept a record of when Sophia was screaming or calling out and the times she would wake and go to sleep.

Rachel advised me to go in when Sophia shouted at bedtime and when she woke too early in the morning. I should tell her she was to settle down to sleep at night, or say that it was too early to get up in the morning. I didn't sit by the bed or cuddle her but I was firm and laid down boundaries for her. This took about two weeks to implement.

By the end of two weeks Sophia was going to bed with no calling out and she was waking any time between 6 and 6:30 a.m. with a little calling out. She now waits until the sun rises on her clock almost every morning before she comes into my room. There is no calling out and she rarely comes to find me before the sun rises on her clock. She is definitely awake before that but she knows she must wait.

Elizabeth

Lucy, my two-year-old, had got used to falling asleep in my arms. I fed her until she was eighteen months old and after that

I used to sing her to sleep. She usually stayed asleep when I transferred her to her cot. This worked in the short term, but if she did wake up while I was transferring her she would cry and sit or stand with her arms out, wanting more cuddles. If she stayed asleep she would often wake later in the evening and be very unsettled. She had never learned how to settle herself.

I tried controlled crying for a week and she did settle more quickly, but then she had chickenpox and was more unsettled at night as a result. I went back to bedtime cuddles and she even ended up in my bed sometimes in the middle of the night when she wouldn't settle in her own room.

I also had an older child, Abigail, and I was worried about Lucy waking her, particularly as she had just started school and was tired in the evenings and mornings. The broken nights were taking their toll on everyone in the family.

Rachel suggested a midway option, which was to have cuddles with Lucy while we said prayers, then transfer her into the cot while singing and while she was still awake, stroking her head while she went to sleep.

I managed to implement this fairly well. Although I was still staying with her, at least she was falling asleep in the cot rather than in my arms, which was a big step forward. And she was old enough to understand when I said that, if she lie down, I would stay with her, but if she didn't lie down, I would have to go out of the room.

Within a few days, Lucy had got used to the new routine and was able to lie down and fall asleep fairly quickly once she was in her cot. As she got used to falling asleep in her cot, she was more able to settle herself if she woke during the night. When she did need settling after waking up too early in the morning, she sometimes settled in the cot while I stroked her head; at other times, I did need to give her a cuddle.

We did have a couple of setbacks. The hot weather made it much harder for her to settle, as did an episode of head lice recently. But it has been a big step forward.

Sleep solutions: three to four years

I am coming toward the end of the book now and my hope is that you have a child who settles and sleeps well. However, you may be reading this because your three- to four-year-old has never slept well and you and your family are exhausted. Please don't despair if this is the case: it is never too late and there is always a chance to put things right. The older your child is, the more time and effort it may take to help him learn how to settle and sleep well, so do be prepared for this. Try to remember that you are not doing it just for your benefit but for your child's as well, as he needs to sleep in order to grow and develop and thrive. When his sleep problems are sorted out you will all feel the benefit, and may wonder why you didn't tackle them before.

You may also be reading this chapter because your child used to sleep well but has suddenly started making a fuss at bedtime and is waking in the night. This is exhausting for you and the family and you will want to put things right. It is usually easier and quicker to help a child settle down again if he has been a good sleeper in the past.

It is important to be able to talk about the problems you are having with your partner and wider family, and with your health visitor or GP. When you are so tired and sleep-deprived and your energy levels are so low, it is easy to bury your head in the sand. If you are back at work, doing anything about your child's bad sleeping habits can feel like too much of an effort. But don't lose heart: the problems can be sorted out, and it will be worth it. The whole family will benefit from better nights' sleep. Now that your child is old enough to understand, it is important that you talk to him and tell him that you are going to help him to sleep well at night, that you love him and don't like to see him tired and grumpy, and that he will feel much happier and enjoy everything more if he learns to sleep well.

How much sleep does my child need?

By the time your child is three to four years old he will need about eleven hours' sleep a night. You may find that when you put him to bed he doesn't always settle straight away. If he sings or chatters in his cot or bed don't worry; as long as he is happy, just leave him to settle by himself. His body clock should be working well by this age, so that he is ready for sleep at bedtime. However, you may find that in the summer months he wakes early, especially when it gets light by about 5 a.m.

Daytime naps

Your child may have dropped his daytime naps by now, as he is probably at nursery, but you may well find that he needs a rest at the weekends. It is good to develop the habit of a child going to his room and having a rest, even if he doesn't sleep. This gives him a chance to unwind – and gives you a break. This is particularly important if you are out working all the week and up early every morning. Your child doesn't have to have a rest on both Saturday and Sunday, especially if you are going out on one of those days, but do try to let him have a nap on one day if you can. He will probably be very tired by Saturday if he has been out early at nursery all week.

When you take him to his room, read him a story to help him settle, then encourage him to lie down and relax. He may like to listen to a CD. As long as he is having a rest it doesn't matter if he doesn't actually sleep.

If you are a stay-at-home mum then your child may still be having a rest in his room several days a week. This is perfectly OK. If he sleeps for a couple of hours in the day but is not tired at bedtime, cut his daytime sleep down to no more than one hour, so that he is ready for bed later on. Don't let him nap late into the afternoon. Make sure he is awake and up again by 3 p.m. You may find that on some days he doesn't sleep at all but just rests in his room, plays with his toys, and chatters away to himself. It is good for both of you to have some time out.

Coming out of nappies

During this year your child will probably come out of nappies and start being dry at night. It is a good idea to have a plastic sheet in the bed with a draw sheet over the top so that if he has an accident you can take the draw sheet out and don't need to change the whole bed. Always have a clean pair of pyjamas by his bed so that if he wakes in the night because he is wet you can change him quickly and put him back to bed.

Cut down his fluid intake before he goes to bed and ensure he does a wee just before you settle him. This will mean he doesn't go to bed with a full bladder. You may want to lift him and take him to the toilet before you go to bed to help him stay dry for the rest of the night.

Although many children are dry at night before they are four years old, don't worry if your child isn't. Plenty of children carry on wetting the bed for several more years, but they always become dry in the end, unless there is something physically wrong with them. Sometimes bed-wetting lasts until puberty. Do talk to your GP if you are particularly worried, but generally the more fuss you make the worse it can become. A child very rarely wets his bed on purpose and usually desperately wants to be dry at night. Bed-wetting means that it is more difficult to go and stay away from home overnight with friends and family so he will want to be dry as much as you want him to be.

Where to sleep

If you have not already done so, you may now want to move your child into a bed, especially if you need his cot for another baby or he has outgrown it. However, you may find that he gets out of his new bed and won't settle at bedtime, as it is all rather a novelty for him to be free. To try and keep him in bed you can buy bars that will slip in under the mattress. Or you could push his bed up against the wall on one side and use the bars on the other side to stop him falling out during the night. Always go and tuck him in before you go to bed in case he has got out or is sleeping across the bed.

You can make the move to a big bed fun by letting him chose some new bedding and maybe a new cuddly toy. This will help it to feel special. If you have bunk beds, keep your three- to four-year-old in the bottom bunk.

If he is now sharing with an older sibling, you may have fun and games getting them to settle at night if they haven't been sleeping together before. However, it is lovely for children to share a bedroom for a while when they are young. It helps them to bond and learn to share and be kind to each other.When I was growing up I got very used to sharing bedrooms as I was one of six children. Our parents divided us up into twos: two girls, two boys, and two girls – and we all had great fun! Because people in general don't have such large families today this isn't done as much, but I do know of families where all the children are in together and sleep very well. One family I know has three toddlers in their cots all together in one room.They chatter away when they are put to bed and the eldest one sometimes sings nursery rhymes to the others before they all go to sleep. So it can be done.

Twins

You will need to move both twins into beds at the same time, as they usually want to do everything together. Sometimes one twin will settle earlier than the other or one will wake early in the morning and try to wake the other one. If one twin is more wakeful, saying that he will have to sleep in a separate room for a while is sometimes enough to help him settle. However, if there is no improvement, move the more restless twin into another room if you can. Be firm with him and ensure that he stays in his room and understands that you mean business.

Establishing good sleeping patterns

It is so important to establish good sleeping patterns for your children. By the time your child is three to four years old you probably start each day at the same time in the morning, as you may be back at work and your child may be at nursery. It is a good idea to have a regular morning routine in any case. Your child should sleep till about 7 a.m.: 5 a.m. is too early for him to be up and about.

If he consistently wakes early and doesn't resettle but wants to be up and running round the house, you will need to teach him that this is not acceptable. It is not good for him or for the rest of the family. He will go to nursery exhausted before he has even started the day, and it is not fair on him.

Bedtime needs to be about 7 p.m. If you are on holiday or out and get back late it won't matter if you have the occasional evening when he is later to bed. However, a stream of late nights will probably make your child grumpy and moody and he will find it difficult to settle to anything. Every child needs to have enough sleep. Having a bath every night helps to establish a good bedtime routine, but if you have been out and about and are late back, a quick wash and straight into bed is fine.

Troubleshooting guide to common problems

Early waking

When your toddler wakes up too early, it is obviously more difficult to keep him in bed once he is in out of his cot and in a real bed. He will probably run into your room and jump into your bed thinking he can snuggle up and be with you until it is time to get up. This of course is lovely, but it may set up bad habits in the long term. You may well find that he comes in earlier and earlier until he starts arriving in your bed in the middle of the night. Whenever he comes in to you before it is time to get up, take him straight back to bed and tuck him in. Tell him he has to stay there, as it is not time to get up yet.

If he continually comes back to you, say that you will shut his door if he won't stay in his bed. Often that is enough to make him stay there. If you don't want to shut his door, you can use a stair gate at the doorway, but he will probably climb over it. If he comes into your bed after you have warned him that you will shut his door, then carry out the plan and shut it. He may shout, but he may settle down straight away.

Sometimes children curl up by the door and go to sleep. If this happens, push the door very gently to open it, then pick him up and tuck him back in his bed.

As your child gets bigger he can open doors and be straight back into your room again. It is important that you do have a boundary that he cannot cross, so you have to be really firm on this and keep putting him back to bed again and again. This may take several weeks of training, or it may succeed quite quickly. Sometimes it will work well at first, then he starts waking early and disturbing you again. If this happens, you will need to start again.

As with any form of sleep training, the important thing is to be consistent and persevere. In the end you will get there and your child will love and respect you for what you are teaching him to do. It is important that your child learns to wait until you are ready for him. You will find that if you persevere with this method, after a while he will probably start sleeping later in the mornings as he knows he is not going to be got up!

It is helpful to leave a couple of little books and a teddy or favourite cuddly toy at the bottom of his cot or bed before you go to bed. This will give him something else to think about and will help him to resettle himself.

Don't give him a drink or food, unless he is ill and needs a drink of water.

Some parents use a small light on a timer that you set to come on at the time he is allowed to get up. Or you can buy a rabbit clock whose ears pop up when it is time for your child to get up. Both of these can work quite well, but you may find that the novelty wears off after a while.

At weekends you can be more relaxed about getting up times, and allow cuddles and stories and chat in bed with your child before you both get up. These can be very special times.

Not settling at bedtime

Not settling to sleep at bedtime is a common problem, but it does need to be sorted out. It is important that your child has plenty of exercise and fresh air during the day so that he is tired and ready for bed. Don't let him have a late afternoon nap or he will not be ready to settle and sleep at bedtime.

After he has had his tea, take him for his bath and make sure you spend a little time playing with him if you can. Dress him in his nightclothes, read him a story and tell him that he is going to bed and is going to settle down and sleep. Talk about the fun things he may be doing the next day, and explain that he needs to go to sleep so that he will have lots of energy tomorrow. Tuck him in bed, kiss him good night, and leave the room.

If he doesn't want you to go away and leave him, tell him that you are not far away. Explain that you are going to tidy the bathroom then you are going to get supper. If he settles with his door open, leave it open until he has gone to sleep, then pop up and close it. Sometimes children go through a phase of being frightened of the door being shut and want a light on outside their room. If this helps him to settle, it's worth doing as it will only be a phase and may not last long.

If he won't settle with his door open, use the same methods as described in the early waking passage to ensure that he stays in his room.

Do talk to your child and explain that what he is doing makes you sad and that the family will be happier if he goes to sleep. Tell him that everyone has to sleep. It may help to use a star chart or reward system of some kind to encourage him to settle and sleep. Children will often get very excited about this as they are normally very competitive and love to do well.

Not sleeping through the night

If your child has never slept through the night then it is a good idea to teach him before he starts school at the age four or five. You may find you have a bit of a battle on your hands, but do persevere and be consistent.

When he wakes in the night, go to him and comfort him, but don't get him out of bed or give him a drink unless he is distressed and needs a cuddle. If he is waking out of habit, then do be firm. After giving a cuddle, tell him he is not coming out of bed, tuck him in, and leave the room, shutting the door if necessary. Leave him to have a shout for about ten minutes, then go back in and say that he is not getting up and must go to sleep. Then leave the room.

You may find this goes on for a couple of hours until he finally falls asleep, either in his bed or curled up by the door. Lift him gently, put him back into his bed, and tuck him in.

You may find you need to do this for several nights, and it may take two weeks or more to work, but I would encourage you to persevere, as the whole family will benefit from having a child who sleeps through the night.

If he has been awake a long time in the night he may sleep later in the morning. If you don't have to get him up for nursery, let him sleep for a half hour or so longer than you would normally let him.

Good sleeper starts waking again

Your child may have been a really good sleeper but has started waking up in the night and finding it difficult to settle to sleep again. This is quite common as a child gets older. He is taking in more and more information and sometimes his little brain doesn't seem able to switch off. He might be having vivid dreams, he may have started school, or have been ill, or there may have been an upset in the family. It is important that you go to him and cuddle him and reassure him, then tuck him up so that he can go back to sleep. If night waking becomes a habit you may have to use one of the sleep training methods discussed in previous chapters. However, it might be a phase that will pass very quickly. Your child is more likely to settle if he has been a good sleeper before.

Going to bed late

Lots of children don't go to bed early enough and their parents really struggle with bedtime. Usually this is because a child has never had a good bedtime routine, but it can happen if there is a family trauma and the child is very unsettled and uncertain of what is happening around him. Try bringing bedtime earlier by fifteen to twenty minutes each night so that you gradually alter your child's body clock. This will be easier for him than suddenly going to bed two or three hours earlier than he has become used to. Aim to get him in bed by 7 p.m. You should be able to achieve this within about a week.

Nightmares, night terrors, sleepwalking

If your child has nightmares, do comfort him. Take him on your lap and cuddle him until he settles down again. Children don't always want to talk about their dreams in the night so don't insist he tells you what the problem is. He just needs your reassurance and love. Once he has calmed down, tuck him back into bed, stroke his head, and tell him you love him. He may settle but wake later in the night. Do the same thing again, affirming him all the time.

When a child has a night terror he will scream out loudly: he is frightened, even though he is not awake. Go to him and take him on your lap and cuddle him. Don't try to wake him up if he is not too distressed. Usually he will settle back to sleep again quite soon, but he may wake again during that same night. He may not remember anything about it the next day.

If your child starts sleepwalking, it is a good idea to put a stair gate at the top of the stairs and make sure there aren't any windows open that he could get out of. When you hear him get up, go to him and gently lead him back to bed. He probably won't wake up and may not remember anything about it the next morning.

Illness and tiredness in the day

If your child has been ill and had disturbed nights he will probably be tired in the day. Do let him nap in the day until he is better. When children are ill they need sleep to help repair their little bodies.

When he is ill and wakes at night, comfort him and offer a drink of water, especially if he has had a raised temperature. He may need medication as well. If he naps in the day, try to get your feet up too if you can, especially if you have other children or a new baby.

Starting preschool

When your child starts preschool he may well be very tired. He may need a good nap in the day sometime during the week. He may also start waking at night but this is a common phase: he probably just wants you to comfort and reassure him. If it is a real problem, do talk to his teacher or carer at school and see if there are things going on there that may be upsetting him. Children don't always come home and tell you everything, so you may have to ask.

A new baby

A new baby in the home will often cause an older child to start having bad nights. He may hear you when you get up to feed the baby in the night, then he may get into a habit of waking and thinking he can be up with you while you feed. He may be jealous of the attention you give the baby. Explain kindly to him that baby needs to feed in the night because he is so little, but he needs to sleep at night like a big boy. Tell him that he can have some special time with you in the morning. Be consistent and persevere.

Life changes

If you have a trauma going on in the home, like a bereavement or relationship breakdown, this is likely to upset your child. He may start waking in the night and being very distressed. The only thing you can do is to love him through it, give him lots of cuddles, and talk to him about it. There is no easy way through this and you will need support from your family and friends to help you through.

Hospitalization

If your child has been in hospital it may be difficult to get him back into a good sleeping pattern when he comes home. He will have had lots of attention while he has been ill, and rightly so, but you will need to gently establish the boundaries again, with lots of chatting and telling him that you love him. It is important that you reaffirm your love and care to him: he needs to feel safe and secure.

Holidays and time zones

If you travel with your child, make sure he has plenty of fluids and snacks and meals while travelling. Let him nap when he needs to on the journey. When you arrive, if he is very tired let him have a sleep to catch up, and give him something to eat. Gradually that day start having your meals at the local time, then put him to bed in the evening, perhaps a little later than usual. Do remember that he may not sleep well the first night and may be up very early next morning. He may need a nap in the day, but by the second evening he should be ready to settle for bed. You may find that he adapts very quickly to a different time zone – children usually do.

A change of routine or time zone during a holiday often causes a child to have disturbed nights when they get back home. You need to be patient but firm and re-establish good sleep patterns for your child. He will soon settle down again, particularly if he was a good sleeper before. If he has a history of sleep problems you may find that it takes several weeks for him to settle down to sleeping well. You may need to use one of the sleep training methods described earlier.

Sleep diary

If you are struggling to get your child into a good sleep pattern, it is a good idea to keep a diary of when he settles to sleep and how long he sleeps for. This is really to help you see that you are making progress, as when you are up and down at night it is often hard to remember in the morning what happened. If you write down what happens in the night, what time your child wakes and how long he takes to settle, this will show you whether the same thing happens every night.

Case studies

Fiona

My three-year-old daughter refused to go to sleep in her own bed, although she would usually settle on her own in my bed. She was often not tired enough in the evenings, because of having unscheduled late afternoon naps.

I felt that I had no privacy and I wasn't sleeping very well with a small person taking up all the space in my bed. The problem had been going on for a few months.

Rachel advised me not to give in but to keep returning my daughter to her own bed during the night. She suggested that I try a system of rewards and that I curbed the late-afternoon nap by replacing it with a quiet time after lunch. The key thing I took from our discussion was to treat my daughter in an age-appropriate way. I hadn't really thought that she could understand more about consequences, rewards, and incentives at three and a quarter than she could at two and a half.

I found getting my daughter to go to sleep in her own bed fairly easy when I put my mind to it. I used the incentive of keeping a new toy that she had been given out of the cupboard if she went to sleep in her own bed. I let her have the light on and bought a new audio book for her to listen to. Going to bed – and to sleep – in her own bed is now OK if she is tired enough.

Getting her to stay in bed all night has been more difficult. She seems to stir at some point every night. If she stirs before I go to bed, I can generally settle her in her own bed. If not, she seems to wake at some point and come in to me. I have not found the energy or determination yet to make her stay in her own bed in the middle of the night!

The late nap issue has not been fully solved. I've not managed to use the after-lunch "quiet time" idea, mainly because she is not in the same place every day. My mum has been very good at trying to keep her going while I am at work – giving her an early tea and then taking her to the playground or other outdoor activities rather than letting her slump in front of the television in the late afternoon. When she doesn't have a late-afternoon nap, she is often asleep within minutes of going to bed. If she has had a late nap, she often goes to bed like a good girl but genuinely cannot get to sleep so ends up being awake until I go to bed.

We had a little setback when we stayed the night at a friend's house and shared a bed, so she wanted to go in my bed when we got home.

On a good day when everything goes to plan, we have a lovely full day, she has a bath and is in bed by 7 p.m. She is often asleep by 7:15 p.m. I then have an evening to myself to relax or to do chores and all is well.

Sleep solutions:
four to five years

When your child gets to between four and five years of age you will realize that you no longer have a toddler but a little person who has a mind of his own and a real personality. You can have lovely conversations with him and he will be able to express his own opinions. He will be interested in what is going on around him and will get upset when he sees friends or family members in trouble. He will be going to school full time by the time he is five years old, if not before. It is so important that he sleeps well at night, as if he doesn't he will be constantly tired and find it difficult to thrive at school.

If you are having problems with him going to bed and sleeping right through the night, you can talk to him about it and he will understand what you are saying. Sit him down, give him a cuddle, and chat with him about why he doesn't settle and what makes him wake up in the night.

How much sleep does my child need?

Most children of this age need about eleven hours' sleep a night. However, some children don't seem to need as much sleep as others and will thrive on ten hours a night. You may find that on some nights your child sleeps longer than others. It is still important to put your child to bed at about 7 p.m. on most nights. If he is late going to bed night after night he will be tired and grumpy.

Daytime rests

Your child will only need a daytime rest or nap at the weekend if he has got very tired with school and activities during the week. He may just need to go into his room and have some quiet time with a book or CD, to help him wind down. This also gives you as parents a chance to have some quiet time, especially if you are both working long hours. If your child has been ill and up in the night, this is another good reason for him having a daytime nap or quiet time.

Establishing good sleeping patterns

Good sleeping patterns can make all the difference to family life. Overtired parents and children really suffer and find it difficult to enjoy life.

Start your child's bedtime routine in plenty of time so that no one feels rushed. Your child always knows when you are in a hurry, and this will tend to make him play up more.

Tell your child that it is soon going to be time to get ready for bed, take him to have a bath or a wash, and get his nightclothes on. By now your child will be able to undress and dress himself, even if it takes a while. Some children want to do it themselves, whereas others need some coaxing and encouragement to get on with it. Give your child a bath every night if you can, but if that's not possible, don't worry.

Spend some time with your child while he is in the bath, playing with him and chatting about his day and your day and what the family has been doing. If daddy is around, children often love it if he does bath time. Get your child out of the bath, sit him on your lap, and while you are drying him give him a cuddle and chat to him. Then take him to his room, read him a story, and give him time to wind down with you before you put him to bed. Remember that children of this age always want "just one more story", so decide in advance how many stories you are going to read and stick to it. It's not a good idea to let your child watch TV after his bath, as he needs to settle down and not be overstimulated. Help him to clean his teeth and make sure he does a wee just before he gets into bed.

Tuck him in bed and kiss him good night. Give him a hug and leave the room. He may be at the stage when he needs a little light on if he is frightened of the dark, or he may want you to leave his door open as he then feels you are not too far away. Both of these things are fine as long as he settles and doesn't keep coming out of his room wanting things.

If your child is very reluctant for you to leave him, tell him that you are not far away. You are just going to tidy the bathroom or get a meal ready. If he settles with his door open, wait until he is asleep, then close it.

Siblings sharing a bedroom

If you have several children your eldest may well be sharing a room with a sibling. You may find that your five-year-old needs to stay up for another twenty minutes or so while the younger child settles to sleep. You could allow the five-year-old to look at a book downstairs while the younger child settles. However, some children settle well together and will just chat for a little while and then go to sleep. It is lovely for children to share a bedroom and good for them to learn to share their space and toys and to look after each other. Bunk beds are useful if you are short of space but make sure your older child goes on the top bunk just in case the younger one falls out.

Dry at night

If your child is not yet dry at night, don't worry about it. Some children are not dry at night until the age of five, and even when they are, they may still have accidents. Often they will wet the bed when they start school or if they are unsettled about something. The most helpful thing for a child who is wet at night is for his parents to be relaxed about it. He will hate having a wet bed and certainly doesn't wet out of naughtiness. So do give him time, and lots of love and assurance that he will get through this.

It is important to keep his fluid intake down before bedtime. I've always found it useful to lift a child to do a wee before you go to bed at night. Don't worry that you will wake him by doing this. More often than not a child will tuck down into bed and go straight back to sleep after being lifted.

Of course if you are worried about anything specific, talk to your health visitor or GP.

Twins

You may find you have one twin who sleeps really well and one who finds it difficult to settle. Putting them in separate rooms may help. Very often, just the idea of being separated will sort the problem out, as they will inevitably want to be together. If this is not practical, be firm with the wakeful one and and explain to the other one that his brother or sister has to learn to go to sleep. Usually twins are very good at sleeping through each others' noises.

Night lights

A child of this age may be frightened of the dark and think that he can see monsters in his bedroom. It is a good idea to let them have a night light in their room or leave their door open slightly so that they can see the light on outside their room. This is a phase and will pass, but it can be very real to a young child, so do be sensitive to him.

Common sleeping problems and solutions

There are many reasons why a child who has slept well will suddenly start waking in the night. The most common of these is starting school. It is a big step for a child to go to school and stay there all day. Although he may have settled in well and be happy during the day, at night he may wake and be quite distressed. Often this is because he is on the go all day and his little head is so full of new things that when he sleeps he has vivid dreams. Or he may enter a light sleep and feel uncertain about things, so he wakes up and cries.

It is important to talk to him about this if it is becoming an issue. Explain that you are there and you love him and he doesn't need to be frightened or worried about school. He may be finding it difficult to make friends and this may be on his mind.

When he wakes in the night, go in to him, cuddle him, give him a drink of water if that helps, reassure him, and tuck him back into bed. If he continually wakes and cries, go back each time and reassure and give him a cuddle. You may find that he settles if you sit by his bed for a few minutes stroking his head. Don't wait till he falls asleep, just quietly leave the room. This may be the best way to help him settle when he is sharing a room with other siblings, as you don't want them woken as well. However, it is amazing how well children can sleep when another child is awake and crying nearby.

Make sure that your child knows that he must stay in bed and go back to sleep. Do talk to him about it in the daytime to help him to understand that you want him to sleep well at night. Tell him that he will feel much happier and better in the morning if he does. So, persevere and be consistent in what you do, and night-time waking will pass and he will settle back into a good sleep pattern.

On the other hand, you may find that your child sleeps better once he starts school, as he is so busy and active during the day that he is very ready for bed in the evening.

Difficulty settling at bedtime

There can be all sorts of reasons why a child is difficult to settle at bedtime. Sometimes it is because he is desperately overtired and just can't wind down. This can sometimes happen when he starts school, or because of illness or trauma at home.

Sometimes it is good if he goes to his bedroom after tea and plays with his toys. Some children relax by watching television or a DVD, but this can overstimulate other children and they make a fuss when you need to turn it off.

If your child is really tired from a day at school, start bath time and bedtime a little earlier so that neither of you feels rushed. This may not be easy if you have a toddler and/or a baby to bath as well. If this is the case, do involve your five-year-old in helping you with the other children. He may be able to do little errands for you or keep an eye on the baby for a minute. You may find it is easiest to put all the children in the bath together as they often enjoy that and it can help stop any tears or temper. This can be the most stressful time of the day, however, as everyone is tired and fractious.

Reading a story to a child will help him to wind down. Put him in bed, then sit on the bed with him and read so that he can look at the pictures with you. Tell him how many stories you are going to read, and stick to it. When you have finished, tuck him in, kiss him good night, and leave the room. If he comes out of his room or uses delaying tactics, be firm. Take him back to bed and only let him have one more drink, or one more wee, and then settle him down again.

If he comes out again, be firm, put him back in his room, and tell him that you will shut the door. If he still comes out, shut the door. If he continues to run in and out, keep putting him back to bed. This may go on all evening, but do persevere as eventually he will be so tired that he will flop into bed and sleep. You may have to do this night after night for several days or even weeks before he learns that you mean business. It is exhausting; but it is so important that you lay down these boundaries. He will love you and respect you much more than if you just let him have his way. When you are exhausted, the easy way is to give in and let him run around, but you are not doing him any favours in the long run.

New baby in the home

This is another common reason why a child will start waking at night. However, by the time a child is five he may be old enough to accept the new baby without feeling any jealousy. If he does start waking when you bring baby home, it may be because he hears you getting up to feed baby in the night. Take him back to bed and tuck him in, telling him that you love him lots but baby needs a feed. Don't let him sit up with you while you feed the baby as this will become a difficult habit to break and is no good for your child as he will be tired next day. Do talk to him and explain that he needs to sleep at night as he is a big boy and not like a baby who needs a feed in the night.

Illness, hospitalization

Your child will have disturbed sleep patterns if he has been ill or in hospital and you may have to teach him how to settle and sleep again. Always show lots of love and understanding, but do be firm as he will, quite rightly, have had lots of extra attention when he was ill. As soon as he is well again, use the methods in this book to sort out any problems with settling to sleep or night waking. If your child was a good sleeper before his illness then he will probably soon slip back into good sleeping patterns again.

Life changes

Bereavement or family breakdown will have an effect on your child and cause him to be unsettled. Your child may suddenly find he is spending time with one parent during the week and the other parent at weekends. If this is happening to you, give your child lots of love and time. Let him talk about how he feels. You may well find that he is upset at night and finds it difficult to settle to sleep.

A young child will often want to talk, then when you have listened to him and reassured him, he will run off and play and apparently forget all about it.

If you are facing any trauma in the home, it is so important to show love and affection to your child and to give him the stability that he needs.

Coming into your bed at night

If your child starts coming into your bed at night, take him straight back to his own room. Take him to do a wee if he needs to, otherwise pop him back in his bed, tuck him in, give him a cuddle, and leave the room. Each time he comes in to you take him straight back to bed telling him you will shut his door if he comes out again. This may be a good enough deterrent to stop him and he may settle back to sleep quickly.

If he is distressed you may have to sit with him for a little while in his room, stroking his head. When he is sleepy, leave the room quietly.

If he is running in and out and being naughty, every time he comes in take him back to bed and tell him he is to stay there. Leave the room and shut the door. You may find you have to do this for several hours and you will be exhausted, but it is worth it in the end. You may find that he learns quickly and in a few days he sleeps through without disturbing you, but you may find it takes several weeks to teach him to stay in his own bedroom.

Nightmares, sleepwalking, and night terrors

Many children have bad dreams and nightmares and this can be disturbing for everyone. Normally by the time your child is about six years old he will have grown out of them. Go to him when you hear him cry out, give him a cuddle, and settle him back down to sleep. You may need to take him on your lap and cuddle him into you and reassure him that you are there. He may genuinely believe that there is a monster in his room or his bed. He might want a little drink of water so you could keep one in his room if he is constantly waking in the night with bad dreams.

He will probably settle down again quite quickly, even though he may wake again in a little while with another bad dream. Try not to discuss the dream unless he wants to talk about it. Most children will have forgotten all about it when morning comes.

He may sleepwalk and wander around in the night while he is asleep. Do make sure there is a stair gate to prevent him from falling down the stairs, and make sure he can't fall out of a window. When you hear him, go to him and gently lead him back to bed. He will probably snuggle down straight away. If he sleeps in a top bunk, move him so that when he does sleepwalk he is safe and won't fall out of bed.

When a child has a night terror he will scream out loudly, as he is frightened even though he is not awake. Go to him and take him on your lap and cuddle him. Don't try to wake him up if he is not too distressed. Usually he will settle back to sleep again quite soon, but he may wake again during the same night. He may not remember anything about it the next day.

Early waking

If your child starts to wake too early in the morning, perhaps in summer when it gets light so early, be firm. If he needs to do a wee, let him, but then put him back to bed. Every time he comes out of his room, take him back again and tell him it is not time to get up. Close his door when you leave his room.

If he keeps waking up too early, he will be very tired at night.

You may like to set a clock alarm in his room that doesn't go off until you want him to get up. This can be a child's clock or a light on a timer if your child hasn't learned to tell the time yet.

Very often, giving rewards will encourage a child to stay in his room. Make sure that you don't give the reward too soon, as he needs to succeed at what you are teaching him for about a week.

If he is very tired at night and has been going to bed early you may want to shift his bedtime back to where it was. Explain to him that he can stay up later at night if he stays in his bed in the morning. You may find that by having a slightly later bedtime he sleeps longer in the morning, but don't be tempted to push bedtime much later than 7:30 p.m.

Coming into your bed in the morning

It is lovely for your child or children to come into your bed when it is time to get up and have cuddles and a story, but it is best only to allow this at weekends as a treat.

Late bedtimes

If your child goes to bed as late as 9 or 10 p.m. every evening, he will be constantly tired. The best way to sort this out is to bring his bedtime forward every night by twenty minutes or so over a period of one to two weeks. This gradual process enables his body clock to adjust to the new bedtime.

You will need to be firm and explain to him that you want him to have a good night's sleep so that he can be happy and go to school and play with his friends. This may take some perseverance if he is used to being up with you all the evening.

Use a rewards system or find something that he really wants to do or to have and use that as an incentive for going to bed at about 7 p.m.

Holidays and time zones

If you travel with your child, make sure he has plenty of fluids and snacks on the journey. Let him nap when he needs to, and when you arrive at your destination let him have a sleep if he is very tired. During the first day, gradually adjust mealtimes to the local time, then put him to bed in the evening. Remember that he may not sleep well the first night and may be up very early the next morning. He may need a daytime nap the following day, but by the second evening he will probably be ready to settle for bed at his normal time. Children often adapt more quickly than adults.

Sleep diary

If you are really struggling with getting your child to settle and to sleep at night it is a good idea to use a sleep diary. It is difficult to remember exactly what happened in the night when you are very tired. Write down the time he goes to bed, how long it takes him to settle, how long he sleeps for, and what time he wakes in the night. You will see by this if there is any pattern in his waking in the night and it will encourage you to see the progress he is making.

Case studies

Rosa

When my older son Stephen was five and a half he was a very early riser, waking most days between 5 and 5:15 a.m. He would make a lot of fuss and wake the whole house up, including my younger son, who was one year old. Stephen was exhausted and prone to tantrums, and lack of sleep was making me short tempered. Guy, the baby, was beginning to copy his older brother's sleep pattern.

Stephen had always been an early riser, but until he was about four and a half he would stay in bed until 6 a.m.

Because his early waking meant he was going to bed early too, at 6 p.m., Rachel suggested that I gradually move Stephen's bedtime towards 7 p.m. She said it was important that I made Stephen feel that he was the "grown-up" brother and that he should be going to bed later than the baby was. She also suggested I lift Stephen before I went to bed.

I was able to start making changes straight away. Lifting Stephen was the hardest part of the advice to follow, as physically moving him is a challenge – he is quite long and rather heavy and I'm quite small. I also have to be careful as both he and Guy are light sleepers.

It took time for the new system to work. Stephen seems to need exactly eleven hours' sleep, so until we managed to get his bedtime to 6:45 p.m. it was still a bit painful in the morning. I also had to come down hard on him making multiple trips to the loo at the crack of dawn and wandering in and out of my room. I had originally allowed him to read until 6 a.m., when he could get up, but I realized pretty quickly that this was a bit of a game to him, and he wasn't making any effort to go back to sleep if he stirred early. I had to take his side-light out of his bedroom at one point as he was completely worn out by his enthusiasm for early morning book-browsing!

Stephen now goes to bed at 6:45 p.m. He says he is woken by our boiler, which comes on at 5:45 a.m. We all need to be awake for the work and school runs at 6 a.m., so this is just about OK. Stephen has become really great at waiting until he hears my alarm before coming into my room in the morning.

Oddly, to begin with, the biggest problem was Guy, the baby. He was upset by the change of routine at bedtime, and evidently missed having his brother around at the start of his sleep time. I fixed this by bathing them together for a few days, then letting Stephen come down in his PJs for a bit of grown-up time.

Adjusting Stephen's routine so that he doesn't get up quite so early has made a massive difference to family life. It was becoming almost impossible to cope with the early starts, combined with the usual broken nights you associate with having a young baby in the house. I had stopped going out in the evenings as I had to go to bed by 9 p.m. in order to get enough sleep. And I was constantly shouting at Stephen and was in danger of not being able to see when he was being a good boy. It's great to start the day now with a hug, not a moan or a shout.

Claire

My problem was that Flora, my five-year-old, had got into a pattern of falling asleep while listening to a bedtime story. She got very upset if she was still awake (or if she woke up) when I left the room.

When Flora was a baby, I had taught her to settle herself through controlled crying, which had worked well. When I moved her into a different room and a big bed just before her third birthday (and before the arrival a couple of months later of her baby sister), she was a bit unsettled. I started staying with her for a time while she fell asleep – and somehow, two years on, that was still the case. Typically I read four stories and she closed her eyes for the last two. There was one book that almost always sent her off to sleep, but if it failed to do its job, Flora got very upset if I left the room before she was asleep. Bedtime could take a very long time, which was frustrating for everyone.

When Flora started school and was tired anyway after a busy day, I realized I needed to sort out bedtime and make it more manageable so that she could get to sleep more quickly.

Following Rachel's advice, I talked to Flora about being a big girl and not needing to fall asleep to stories anymore. I started by cutting back the stories from four to two. We often read the first one snuggled in bed together, followed by prayers. Then I read the second one sitting by the bed, with Flora lying down with her eyes closed. She was quite often asleep before the end of the second story. If she was still awake, I encouraged her to look at a book on her own quietly and told her I would come back in five minutes to turn off the light.

She was a bit unsure to start with, but the rewards chart helped. A couple of nights into the new routine her dad was away and the baby was taking a while to settle, so I asked Flora to sit in her bed and wait for me to come through. By the time her sister was settled, Flora had fallen asleep by herself. This happened on a couple of other occasions, and each time Flora was praised and had a star on her chart.

The key thing is that she now knows that she can settle herself, which takes the fear out of being left in her room alone and awake. Although she often falls asleep during the second story, she knows she doesn't need to worry if she doesn't. It has made the whole bedtime experience so much more peaceful.

The spiritual and emotional needs of your child

As I write this chapter I'm sailing down the River Rhine on a cruise, a much-needed holiday. We are sailing through some beautiful countryside with wooded banks and hillsides filled with vineyards. All this makes me think about God, the creator of the universe, and his amazing love, care, and provision for us all. I write as a Christian and hope you will find this chapter a comfort and help wherever you are in your journey of faith.

Why am I writing this chapter in a book on sleep? In the book I've talked lots about boundaries, teaching children how to sleep, and the process of sleep training, and whether it feels right or wrong to let a child cry. I want you to look at your baby or child as a whole person. Children are not robots but are precious gifts from God. As a gift from God, each child needs to be treasured, cherished, and nurtured. You may be finding the process of dealing with sleep problems very emotionally draining and I hope this chapter will be a help to you.

Prayer in everyday life

Let me tell you about my own children. When they were newborn I would pray over them in their cots at night when I settled them down to sleep, asking God's blessing and safekeeping on them. I would also hold them close to me and sing to them and pray for them. I have found when working with families that if a baby is highly strung or overtired and unable to sleep, it really helps to hold him tight into my shoulder and sing and pray. This nearly always calms him so he will be able to settle and sleep.

If you haven't prayed before, don't worry, it needs only to be a few simple words, such as "Please God, look after my precious baby and keep him safe tonight. Amen".

As babies become toddlers, prayer and stories can become a lovely part of their bedtime routine. As they get older they can learn to put their little hands together and close their eyes. Often I will sit a young toddler on my lap and he'll put his hands together and close his eyes while I pray, then I give him a big cuddle and put him in his cot.

As your toddler begins to speak and respond he will often begin to name family members and even pets in his prayers. I have known young children to get quite carried away when praying for many different people and things, so you may find you have to gently bring him to a close! Teaching children that there is a greater being than them can really help them to feel secure and protected.

As well as praying with your child, reading Bible stories can also provide comfort and reassurance for your child as part of his bedtime routine. Children often have a favourite book or story that they like to read each night.

Prayer can be really helpful for older children if they wake in the night frightened by a bad dream. You can cuddle them, pray with them, and ask God to take away the fear and help them to go back to sleep. This can be a great comfort to a child. I have experienced this recently with one of my grandchildren, who went through a period of having bad dreams and thinking there was a monster in the room. He would call out in the night, "Please Gangan, will you ask Jesus to take the monster away?" I would pray with him and this would help him to lie down and feel peaceful again.

Prayer and spirituality in difficult times

As parents, we can feel we are living on the edge if we are sleep deprived and struggling with daily life. I've found that prayer has been a great help and comfort to me in those times. For me, to have an awareness of God who cares for me and loves me, and is concerned about my everyday needs, has always been a source of strength in difficult times.

If you are struggling and don't know who to turn to, many toddler groups are run by churches and there will often be someone there who will be happy to talk to you and pray with you.

In family life we can experience serious challenges and losses. Faith sadly does not protect us from difficult circumstances, but leaning on God and on each other can help to carry you through. As a family you will need much support if you are going through bereavement, serious illness, family breakdown, unemployment, or financial difficulties. In these circumstances you need friends and family around you who can provide both practical and emotional support. If you feel isolated, often a local church will provide friendship, support, and prayer during these times.

A very common challenge in family life, particularly if your baby is not sleeping well, is postnatal depression. Seeking help and talking about how you are feeling is vital. Do seek professional advice from your health visitor or GP. An awareness of God and his love and care can also be a great help, as well as praying for your child when you are feeling in the depths of despair. If you feel you just can't pray, it can really help to ask friends and family to pray for you and your baby. It is natural to feel that God has left you, or that there is no God at these times, and you need to lean on others. It can also help just to hold on to the fact that God's character is love, and he loves you deeply.

Conclusion

As I come to the end of the book, my prayer is that it will have been a real help and encouragement to you. I hope that through the advice I have given, your baby or child will begin to be a really good sleeper. I trust that you have found this book a comfort and a guide.

A prayer for you

Now I lay me down to sleep,
I pray the Lord, my soul to keep;
Guide and guard me through the night
And wake me with the morning's light.

Index

Further information

For more information on topics such as feeding and enjoying your baby and toddler, see Rachel's other books, *The Baby Book: How to Enjoy Year One*, and *The Toddler Book: How to Enjoy Your Growing Child*. Both are published by Lion Hudson. Rachel can be contacted via her website: *rachelsbabies.com*.